TEACHING EXCE

Cases for Refle

for

Exceptional Learners
Introduction to Special Education

SEVENTH EDITION

Daniel P. Hallahan
University of Virginia

James M. Kauffman
University of Virginia

Allyn and Bacon
Boston · London · Toronto · Sydney · Tokyo · Singapore

ISBN 0-205-27142-1

Printed in the United States of America

10 9 8 7 6 5 4 3 2 1   01 00 99 98 97 96

Table of Contents

Preface

Preface

The cases we have selected for inclusion in this booklet reflect both the joy and the pain of teachers working with exceptional children. What professors of education and commentators in the popular press write about teaching is often wondrously abstract, hypothetical, or idealistic, and does not ring true for those who work daily in classrooms. In contrast, the stories we call cases are neither abstract descriptions nor conjecture, nor do they reflect an idealism detached from the realities of the classroom. They are true stories of teachers--what really happened as told from the perspectives of real teachers and how they thought and felt about what was happening.

Because of the sensitive nature of much of the information contained in most of the cases, the identities of the teachers who wrote them, as well as the other individuals who are described in their stories, must inmost cases be masked. We are grateful to Susan Washko and to the other teachers identified by pseudonyms who told us or wrote the stories comprising these cases. Their willingness to share their experiences has given many other educators priceless opportunities to reflect on the art and science of teaching exceptional children. We are also grateful to the Commonwealth Center for the Education of Teachers and its director, Robert F. McNergney , for support of our work in obtaining and writing the cases.

D. P. H.

J. M. K.

Charlottesville, Virginia

INTRODUCTION

This is a collection of cases for use as a supplement with our text, *Exceptional Learners: Introduction to Special Education* (Hallahan & Kauffman, 1997). Some are cases we have written following interviews with teachers, others were written by teachers or intern teachers themselves. All the cases are factual -- they are not hypothetical, and the only changes in the facts of the cases are those necessary to protect the identities of the individuals about whom they are written.

Background

The use of cases in teaching has a long, celebrated history in law and business. Some schools, for example the Harvard Business School and the Darden School of Business at the University of Virginia, use cases as their primary method of instruction. Students analyze and discuss real-life situations that have occurred in the world of business or law. It may be that they address issues surrounding the merger of two Fortune 500 companies, or perhaps they consider the ramifications of an American manufacturing business attempting to open up a market in a foreign country. Whatever the focus of the case, the idea is to get students to consider issues that they are likely to face when they finish their academic work and enter the real world of business.

There is a small, but rapidly growing, number of teacher educators who have started to use cases with preservice teachers, with the idea in mind of enabling them to grapple with issues before they enter the real world of teaching in public schools. We are among this group who have been experimenting with case teaching. We are not claiming that all courses in teacher education lend themselves equally to the use of cases, nor do we believe that the case method is every instructor's cup of tea. There is still the need for more traditional formats, such as lectures. In the introduction to special education course, in particular, cases probably cannot provide all of the information that needs to be conveyed. There is reason to believe, however, that cases can serve as a valuable supplement to other forms of classroom instruction.

Rationale

A basic rationale for using cases in teacher education is that it is a way to teach novices to think more like those with more experience and expertise. The case method may be a way of speeding up the socialization process. For several years, James Boyd White, a law professor, has delivered a speech to entering law school students that emphasizes the use of cases in training the "legal mind." Much of what he says holds true for the education profession. One could substitute the word "teacher" for "lawyer" and "education" for "law" in the following quote and depict our view of the value of using cases in teacher education:

> Let me suggest that you regard the law, not as a set of rules to be memorized, but as an *activity*, as something that people do with their minds and with each other as they act in relation both to a body of authoritative legal material and to the circumstances and events of the actual world. The law is a set of social and intellectual practices that defines a universe or culture in which you will learn to function.... Our primary aim is not to transmit information to you but to help you learn how to do what it is that lawyers do with the problems that come to them....
>
> Of course the law as an activity can and should be studied...from the point of view of other disciplines.... But in studying the law in such ways one is functioning, not as a lawyer, but as an anthropologist, as a historian, and so forth. What is peculiar and central to your experience both in law school and beyond is that you learn how to participate in this activity, not as an academic, but as a legal mind....
>
> A[n] analogy [to learning law] may be learning a language. One must of course learn the rules of grammar and the meaning of terms, but to know those things is not to know how to speak the language. That knowledge comes only with use. (White, 1985, pp. 52-53)

Researchers in the area of cognitive science also provide us with grounds to believe that cases can be useful in teacher education. Their research informs us that people learning a complex task (And what could be more complicated than teaching!) learn it best when they can do it under the tutelage of experts whom they can model. In an introductory course to special education, it would not be practical, nor would it be ethical, to have students be responsible for solving real problems presented by students with disabilities. The next best thing, however, is to have students consider cases of teaching situations involving students with disabilities. Discussing cases that require solutions to real problems encountered by real teachers, although a step removed from actually having to solve the problems in the natural setting, should be more helpful in making teachers better problem solvers than teachers trained through traditional lecture and discussion formats. Cases provide a narrative of teachers in action. Discussing cases provides a forum for preservice teachers to try out ideas and potential solutions before actually being faced with making those decisions under fire in the classroom. For the inservice teacher, discussing cases provides the opportunity to hone their decision making skills. In this way, then, a case method can serve as a bridge between academia and the classroom.

The Cases

The cases we have chosen for this supplement involve teachers working with students exemplifying a wide range of ages and disabilities, as well as a case involving students who are gifted. Recognizing that many students who will use this supplement are in general education and that more and more students are spending more and more time in regular classes, the focus of most of the cases is on a teaching situation involving a general education setting. We have provided "Questions for Reflection: with each case that are aimed to help you think about some of the major issues of the case. Whenever possible, we have noted links between these questions and specific chapters in the Hallahan and Kauffman text.

Cautions

We caution that not all of the cases portray best practices or a high level of teacher reflection. It is our experience that it is a rare case that does not contain at least some actions or attitudes of the teacher or teachers that are open to criticism. At the same time, it is a rare case that is totally devoid of good teaching practices. Remember, these are *real* cases, that is, "slices of teaching life." They show teachers in action, in emotionally charged situations that often demand split-second decisions. in fact, by giving you the "luxury: of time to reflect on such cases. we hope we will be helping you become better decision makers when faced with similar circumstances. Finally, we caution you that our "Questions for Reflection" do not necessarily have one right answer. Moreover, answers are not always found in the Hallahan and Kauffman text--or any other book, for that matter. Teaching is not an endeavor for which there is always a textbook description. Like other professions, teaching demands integrating knowledge from a variety of sources to address problems through intellectually rigorous inquiry and ethically defensible action.

References

Hallahan, D. P., & Kauffman, J. M. (1997). *Exceptional learners: Introduction to special education.* (7th ed.). Boston: Allyn & Bacon.

Kauffman, J. M., Mostert, M. P., Nuttycombe, D. G., Trent, S. C., & Hallahan, D. P. (1993). *Managing classroom behavior: A reflective case-based approach.* Boston: Allyn & Bacon.

White, J. B. (1985). *Heracles' bow: Essays on the rhetoric and poetics of the law.* Madison, WI: University of Wisconsin Press.

SHOULD I TAKE JUANITA POPE?

Isabelle Dworkin

During the beginning weeks of school, several sixth grade teachers who worked as a team came to me with a complaint.

"We have a little girl on our unit who *definitely* belongs in your class."

Later, the principal came to me.

"We may have another little girl for you."

Then the head of the child study team came by.

"Don't get too settled with your numbers [of students], because we may be adding one to your class roll. She's already been referred for child study, and I'll let you know when we have her child study meeting."

Well, with all of these people insinuating that a new body would eventually be placed in my classroom, it was definitely time to find out exactly who Juanita Pope was.

During her early school years, Juanita lived with her mother, Mrs. Pope. She never attended preschool. Mrs. Pope claimed that she was not aware that Juanita could come to school when she was six years old. Therefore, Juanita was not sent to kindergarten until she was 6 years, 9 months old. This confused start in school reflects the state of Juanita's educational history.

Her kindergarten teacher felt that Juanita's strengths were in the areas of fine motor development, self-help, and eagerness to try new things. She was weak in the areas of math and language skills. At the time of her initial evaluation, her adaptive behavior scale scores reflected adequately developed socialization, self-help, and receptive language skills. Juanita was weak in expressive and written language skills. The teacher stated that the scores were influenced by

4

"lack of opportunity in the home environment." The eligibility committee decided she was developmentally delayed--25% delayed in communication, daily living skills, and cognition. IQ: 68. Mental retardation was not suspected due to the "inconsistency of the scores." She was placed in a special "multicategorical" class with some mainstreaming.

However, during the next school year, Juanita was beyond the age limit for the multicategorical class, so another child study meeting was held to assess her progress and find another placement. The regular classroom teacher who had her indicated that Juanita was shy and did not ask for help, did well with the "concrete and connecting levels" in math, did not do well with concepts that required making inferences, was successful in a "carefully controlled time period with extra attention," and was not functioning well in the mainstream because her primary deficit was in reading. Eligibility for special education was continued, and she was placed in a self-contained class for students with learning disabilities. IQ: 85.

Juanita was re-evaluated three years later. The fifth grade mainstream teacher observed that mainstreaming had gone really well. Juanita had made progress in working on her own, interpreting what she read, and asking questions about the teacher's expectations. She was still shy and hesitant to form new relationships, relied on familiar friendships, and needed a great deal of structure and repetition. Juanita's special education teacher taught her math and commented that "Juanita is not a risk-taker." She went on to describe Juanita as interacting in socially appropriate ways with others but having trouble sharing and contributing to a small peer group, having difficulty with problem-solving and higher level thinking, needing extra time to formulate responses, and having trouble with newly introduced concepts. The psychologist found her strongest skills to be in rote numerical reasoning and rote auditory memory. Her weaknesses were in the areas of visual-motor and spatial orientation. IQ: 71. The psychologist's recommendation: "Work must be at her ability level and should probably be presented in small doses." He went on to recommend using concrete instructional materials, giving Juanita rationales for learning new information, and providing assertiveness training to improve her personal and academic skills. The evaluating committee determined that Juanita was ineligible for any special services because her aptitude and achievement scores indicated significant improvement.

Juanita had an academic history of being shifted from program to program. She had been shifted around a lot in her personal life, too. Mrs. Britt, her grandmother, was constantly called by the school when Juanita lived with her mother. Mrs. Pope did not respond to or comply with the school's notes or calls. When Mrs. Pope's marriage to Juanita's father ended, the oldest daughter, Sheila (Juanita's half-sister), was "given" to her father's relatives in a nearby town. Before Mrs. Pope left town, Juanita and her older brother were "given" to Mrs. Britt. (Mrs. Britt's home seemed to be the place where all of Juanita's siblings were taken when Mrs. Pope either changed boyfriends or became pregnant again.) Mrs. Pope could not be found for several years; when she was found, she had given birth to another child. By this time, Juanita had already started relying heavily on adults at school for support.

After discovering all of this information about Juanita's dysfunctional family history and ever-changing classroom settings, I was convinced that someone had to stop this chaos. If the sixth grade team had their way, Juanita was about to go through yet another eligibility merry-go-round. We had not reached the half-way point of the first nine weeks, and the sixth grade teachers were already pleading fervently to have Juanita referred to the child study committee. The sixth grade team had solicited my input, so I felt comfortable asking these teachers this question, which had been going through my mind: "How in the world did they know this child's abilities if she had only been in school for such a short time?"

The sixth grade teachers assured me that they had had a very frustrating time trying to instruct Juanita.

"If you'd read her file, you'd understand why we're doing this so early."

I told them that I'd read Juanita's file, but they needed to consider that she had been placed directly into all her regular classes without any type of transition. Regardless of my comment, they continued to push to have a child study meeting. But the meeting did not come about. Because Juanita had been found ineligible for special education services only at the end of the previous school year, the special education coordinator wanted the team to give Juanita some time to make the transition to regular classes. Needless to say, perhaps, they were extremely disappointed in how the "transition" turned out.

The sixth grade teachers who were supposed to be helping Juanita make the transition started visiting me regularly to ask my opinion or complain about any problems they were having with Juanita. Many of these teachers and their students had always acted as if I had a scarlet "R" on my door (for Retarded Classroom), this was indeed a novelty. Most of the time, regular education teachers never asked my opinion about anything academic. Just because I taught retarded students, did that make me retarded, too?

The teachers' complaints were usually about Juanita's poor comprehension and basic skills, her inability to spell, and her disinterest or inability to respond to the challenges of their classrooms. They often reminded me that they had many more kids than I did, so I might not understand the magnitude of the problem. I commiserated with them, but continued patiently to remind them that this was a transitional year for Juanita and that her work needed to be monitored and adjusted according to her abilities. Inevitably, I either looked at their assignments and suggested ways to modify them or went directly to my shelves or file cabinet to substitute high interest-low vocabulary work for the higher level materials they were constantly giving her. Sometimes the teachers resisted modifying the materials because they thought the modifications would take away from the quality of the project.

Several teachers also complained about Juanita's poor coping skills. Her shyness had always been a controlling factor in her academic and social development. They complained that she was usually nonreponsive during guided practice time. If they waited quietly after asking a question, she would eventually respond. However, waiting for the response sometimes slowed down the pace of the class so severely that the other students started getting off task. If they

6

attempted to stimulate an answer, Juanita became nonresponsive. If they gave her constructive criticism, suggestions, or reprimands, Juanita also "shut down" and cried soundlessly. While in this mode, she refused to give any eye contact whatsoever. The teachers said that they attempted to ignore the "shut downs" but reacted to the crying by allowing her to go to the bathroom to dry her tears and get composed. This was not working, because Juanita would then take two periods to come back; she not only failed to complete the assignment but missed hearing other assignments as well. I suggested that they were giving Juanita this message: "Crying gets you time off task and attention from others." To this suggestion they responded, "But I don't have time to deal with it."

Furthermore, Juanita was conveniently leaving her homework at home, bringing it in incomplete or not done at all (her excuse: "My grandmother doesn't know how to do this," or "I had to help take care of my little brother, so I didn't have time to do it"), not writing down assignments, losing study guides for tests, not studying for tests, misplacing books, and missing days of school.

At the beginning of the school year, I had decided to do free tutoring for students who were on free or reduced-price lunches. I told the guidance counselors to assign two to four children to me, and I would tutor them as long as they needed my help. The end of the first nine weeks had come and gone, and no students had been referred to me. The sixth grade team had already told me that Juanita was struggling to keep up with her classmates. So I approached Mrs. Walker, the sixth grade guidance counselor, about getting Mrs. Britt's permission to tutor Juanita. It seemed like the most logical thing to do. The guidance counselor agreed that it was a good idea. Mrs. Britt gave her permission, but was concerned that Juanita would not agree to the decision. Mrs. Walker and I arranged to have Juanita sent to her office to ask Juanita's permission to include her in the tutoring sessions.

Our priority in the meeting was that Juanita feel comfortable staying after school and riding home with me. I had already attempted to establish a relationship with Juanita by talking to her in the hallways and at lunchtime. Many times, Juanita did not acknowledge my presence. She was very cautious about talking in my presence, but I was persistent because Juanita looked so unhappy going down the hallways. This meeting would be an indicator of whether I had earned her trust.

When she came into the office, Juanita looked at me suspiciously. I decided to take my cue from Mrs. Walker. She showed Juanita her grades on the computer and explained that she was doing okay in her exploratory class and math (she had made a C), but was making D's and F's in all of her other classes. Mrs. Walker explained that I had a way of helping her improve her grades. Having been given my cue, I told Juanita about my proposed tutoring session and asked her if she wanted to participate. She said very quitely, "I have to ask my grandmother." Mrs. Walker then chimed in, "Why don't we call her now?" (Neither of us wanted to alienate Juanita by telling her we had already contacted Mrs. Britt.) Juanita listened while Mrs. Walker and I talked to her grandmother. I explained that the tutoring sessions would probably be two or three times a week, 3:30 to 5:00, never on Fridays; some days we might have to make special arrangements if I had a class or meeting, and I would give Juanita a ride home after every session. Juanita talked to her grandmother on the phone, and when she hung up she agreed to comply with Mrs. Britt's wishes.

"But," I emphasized to her, "this is your decision, too. If you make the decision, you'll more than likely stick with it." She nodded her assent, and we decided to start the tutoring that next day!

Juanita's teachers were happy with this arrangement and agreed to give me copies of future study guides, assignments, and the teacher's manual for the textbooks if necessary.

First tutoring session; no Juanita. After a long search, I finally found her dragging her feet down a distant hallway. I encouraged her to speed up, and when she would not I reminded her that the later she came to the tutoring session the longer we would have to stay to make up the lost time. She immediately quickened her pace, but the minute she came into the room she had to get a drink of water and go to the bathroom. I agreed to let her go to the bathroom after we established the rules for the tutoring session. I also clarified that the tutoring sessions started exactly at 3:30, so from 3:15 to 3:30 she should get her drink of water and go to the bathroom. Once inside the classroom, I would have a snack for her. If she came late to the session, we would stay longer to make up the missed time. She mumbled her "Okay" and began taking unorganized materials from her notebook.

The biggest challenge during our subsequent tutoring sessions was getting Juanita to bring in necessary materials to complete her assignments. I met her "I have no homework" with, "Well, practice makes perfect. Let's go over the assignment from the other day."

Usually, a bad day in class was followed by a horrible tutoring session. The first time Juanita did her crying routine with me it was because she wanted me to give her the answers for her assignment. When I told her that her work was being graded, not mine, the tears began. I continued explaining the assignment to her--ignoring the tears--and she interrupted by saying, "My other teachers let me go get water and go to the bathroom when I get upset." My response: "Well, that's inappropriate behavior. You can't solve any problem by crying and drinking water. We have work to do. I have tissues in my classroom, and if you're thirsty, I'll fill a cup with water while you do your assignment."

Well, the quiet tears were replaced with loud wailing and Juanita's demand that she be allowed to leave the room to wipe her face and nose. After I ignored her demands, Juanita tried her "shut-down" routine, and I told her that I was willing to out wait her. She informed me that she was not going to do any more work, and I replied, "Take your time, because your time is my time." After a long pause, she said she wanted to call her grandmother. "The office is locked up now, and so are the telephones," I reminded her. She then "shut down" again, so I simply "shut down" too. I started grading papers and cleaning up my room, and after 20 minutes of silence, she got up and wiped her nose. "What else do I have to do?"

I would love to say that we always ended our sessions on a positive note, but we didn't. Several times she conveniently forgot our session and went home on the bus or refused to continue studying for tests at home. Also, having used "inventive" spellings for most of her elementary school career, she was having a hard time correcting the spelling in her written work, even when she could use a spellchecker. She continued to lose many points on her papers due to misspelled words. I was very frustrated when some of her graded projects were returned to her. I believed that her sixth grade teachers did not consider her "transitional" status when they graded her assignments. When I approached them about this, they asked, "What would the other kids think if they saw Juanita's grade and the poor quality of her assignment?" No amount of explaining how hard she had worked could get them to change the grade. The language arts teacher came by my classroom to report that Juanita had not completed her daily journal pertaining to a book she was reading silently. I tried to explain that there were limitations to my involvement in Juanita's participation. It seemed to me that they had stopped holding her accountable. They were not expressing their expectations to Juanita. I was supposed to take care of that, too!

Several times Juanita commented, "Why should I stay after school with you if I'm still getting C's and D's?" She had a very valid point, I thought, but I could only encourage her to continue coming to our sessions. Without my intervention, those C's and D's would become F's.

Juanita had failed science in two consecutive semesters. Mrs. Walker came to my classroom and asked to place Juanita in my class for science. The science teacher felt that there was no way that Juanita would ever grasp the subject matter. So, the team suggested either placing her in another study hall or my classroom (because I already had a trusting relationship with Juanita). I told the guidance counselor that this was just another excuse for the regular education teachers not to do their job; but, yes, I would take Juanita for science. At least she would be actively involved in a structured learning environment, not just reading another library book.

Looking somewhat relieved, Juanita came into my classroom. Her skills were quite comparable to my students with mild mental retardation. In the beginning, she did not like being separated from her friends and would not participate. But when I made her the leader of a cooperative learning group, she became more involved, answered questions, and made friends.

We continued the tutoring sessions, and she ended the school year barely passing to the seventh grade. She had managed to get through the school year without another child study meeting being called, but I knew that we would have that to deal with the next school year. True to form, the sixth grade teachers had already warned the seventh grade teams about Juanita Pope.

Three weeks of the first nine were allowed to pass before the child study referral was made. Within these three weeks, the seventh grade teachers had come to some definite conclusions. They had already lowered their expectations and placed her in collaborative classes, but she still had very poor basic skills in all areas, and could not comprehend directions and concepts. Juanita had, poor organizational skills, poor peer interactions, a delayed response time, and poor academic and social coping skills. One teacher wrote that she was afraid that Juanita would become "a classic example of a student falling through the cracks" at our school if special services were not reinstated. Juanita was placed in an extra "core" class as an alternative to an "exploratory," a common practice in our school when a student has difficulty in most academic classes. The teacher of the extra core classes did not believe that Juanita was making significant progress because most of her work was of poor quality. Juanita was, as she put it, "spending her time in classes with material that is essentially meaningless to her."

The child study team met and decided to recommend a referral for a special education re-evaluation, have a complete neurological to determine the origin of Juanita's delayed responses, and reduce her academic classes by one.

After the child study team's meeting, I received a visit from the leader of the team. They were searching for some place to put Juanita for that one class. There was no way to reschedule her classes with the other seventh grade team, so they thought of my classroom. Once again, my established, "trusting relationship" was lauded by the regular education teachers. In addition, Juanita was complaining to the seventh grade guidance counselor about having all Caucasian teachers, and they felt that I could provide the African-American influence that Juanita desired. Would I please help them solve this problem?

Were they just feeding my ego, or was it a genuine belief that I could make a difference? Would I once again "save the day" for these regular education teachers, who considered my opinion only when it was time to remove bodies from their classes? Shouldn't these teachers be held accountable for nurturing Juanita's academic development? Couldn't they utilize some of the energy being used to get Juanita out of their classroom to modify her classroom assignments? Or, should I just put these personal feelings aside and put Juanita first?

Questions for Reflection

In what ways does Juanita fit the definition of children "at risk"? Do you think she had a disability (or disabilities)? (Hallahan & Kauffman, Chapter 1)

To what extent do you see evidence that the requirements of IDEA were being met by Juanita's school system? (Hallahan & Kauffman, Chapter 1)

Who do you think should have been responsible for teaching Juanita? To what extent were general and special educators collaborating? What do you see as the central issues in role definitions and expectations of the regular classroom teachers and Isabelle? (Hallahan & Kauffman, Chapters 1 and 2).

Ideally, special and general educators work together to include the student with mild mental retardation (retardation not requiring intensive support services) as much as possible in regular classes. Compare this case to the description by Bruce Wojick and Theone Hug of their collaboration (Hallahan & Kauffman, pp. 136-137). What might Isabelle have done to try to work out such a collaborative arrangement to help Juanita make a successful transition into regular classes? What special problems might she have encountered?

What aspects of this case involve multicultural issues? (Hallahan & Kauffman, Chapter 3)

Whose attitudes and behavior do you find most troubling in this case--Juanita's, the regular classroom teachers', or Isabelle's? Why?

WHO WILL HELP PATRICK?

Candace Keller

The first thing that I remember about Patrick is Sara's story of how his foster mother refused to give him a taste of barbecue ribs as she sat hunkered over the table enjoying her large portion of the steaming pile while Patrick whimpered pitifully at her feet, begging for the taste he would never receive. Food used to manipulate and taunt is a thread running throughout Patrick's story. But I am getting ahead of myself.

Sara was at Patrick's apartment in a federally subsidized housing project to perform developmental testing as part of a large battery of evaluations which would be used to determine whether Patrick qualified for special education services from the public schools. Minutes after leaving the dark apartment, Sara sat in my office, enraged and in tears, describing the horror of observing the interactions between this two-year-old and his foster mother, Margaret. Never had Sara seen interactions marked with such extreme intimidation and so totally devoid of nurturance. Never had she seen a child so unable to relax and smile. These were the first of many tears to be shed for Patrick. And there will be more.

Patrick's birth mother, Debra, was a substance abuser who used both alcohol and drugs during her pregnancy. After Patrick's birth, she roamed the streets of the small midwestern city in which she lived, often carrying him with her and leaving him asleep in alleys while she used whatever was available to get her high. As one of the special education coordinators for the local public schools, I was familiar with her history because two years earlier I had chaired the eligibility meeting for her first child, Sade'. Sade' had been placed in a preschool class for children with disabilities because of her extreme behavior problems, but she was now in the custody of relatives in another state. I knew that before Patrick was born Debra had been taken by her social service worker to a clinic to be voluntarily sterilized but had left through a rear door before the surgery was done. The next time the social worker saw Debra she was visibly pregnant with Patrick.

Patrick lived for his first six months with Debra, who continued to live the life of a street person throughout that time. More than once he was found abandoned and screaming in some dark hall or alley. More than once in the first six months of his life he had to be treated for oozing staph infections on his head and arms. Finally, when Debra was sentenced to a short time in the local jail, Patrick was placed by social services in the home of Margaret, his current foster mother.

Margaret had been recommended to social services by Debra. Margaret, who had been a special education student and an acquaintance of Debra's, had four teenagers of her own and needed the money that social services paid to foster parents, meager though she alleged it to be. When I questioned the caseworker about the suitability of this home for Patrick, she countered with her own question, "Who else will take him?"

Patrick was referred to the public schools for evaluation by a public health nurse, who felt that he exhibited developmental delays. She was particularly concerned about his low weight and speech delays. At Patrick's eligibility, unlike any other that I had chaired in more than a decade as special education coordinator, each evaluator told a similar horror story of the terror that they felt from the somber, frail Patrick in reaction to the orders barked at him by Margaret. Each report reiterated how he sucked three fingers (calloused from the act) and rubbed his head with his other hand while Margaret insisted that he *could* do what he failed to do for the assessor. Only once, in five separately administered evaluations, did he smile--when he threw a ball which was caught laughingly by the evaluator, who praised his fine ball handling ability.

The results of all of the evaluations determined that Patrick was developmentally delayed and impaired in speech and language. The developmental assessment indicated significant delays in the areas of adaptive behavior, communication, and cognitive skills, with some delays in motor skills. The psychological evaluation noted that he had many features associated with fetal alcohol syndrome and that he remained apprehensive throughout the testing period. He responded quickly to inhibitions such as, "Wait a minute!" and acted fearful when Margaret spoke loudly to encourage him to complete a task. Unlike most 26 month olds, he did not respond differentially to praise or encouragement. The skills that he demonstrated placed him at the 19-month-old level, and the psychologist suggested that he appeared to be experiencing considerable sadness, apprehension about others' behavior, and a lack of self-confidence. The speech-language evaluation documented communication skills that were uniformly about one year below the expected level. Discussions with Margaret revealed that Patrick seldom initiated interactions and that when he did, it was nonverbal through pointing and vocalizing by crying. The speech-language pathologist found the extreme harshness of Margaret's interactions with Patrick noteworthy. The sociological evaluation, written after an interview with Margaret, stated that Margaret could benefit from assistance in teaching Patrick some developmental skills and in developing appropriate behavior management strategies. The medical evaluation revealed that, although he was judged to be healthy, he was anemic and his weight fell below the fifth percentile, as did his weight-to-height ratio.

When he was two years and five months old, Patrick was placed in a preschool class for children with disabilities with seven other youngsters served by an experienced preschool special education teacher and an assistant. He quickly became the most challenging student in the class, exhibiting severe mood swings from cooperative to belligerent, from loving to aggressive, from lethargic to tantruming. Patrick was invasive of other students' space, often hitting, pinching, and attempting to bite them. His need for food was often insatiable, with demands for food beginning as soon as he got off of the school bus. During his first year of preschool--February to June--his teachers attempted to manage his behavior by putting him in time out in a playpen when he was hyperaggressive. The entire school was traumatized by loud, piercing screams, sometimes lasting for more than an hour. Aware that the recommended amount of time-out for toddlers is one minute for each year of age, the teacher attempted to limit Patrick's time out in the playpen. However, his aggressive behavior and unwillingness to change often left her with no recourse but to leave him screaming wildly in his playpen so that she could attend to the other students.

The teacher approached Margaret for help in managing this behavior, which was totally unpredictable and seemed clearly out of Patrick's own control. Margaret was extremely critical of the teacher's techniques and offered the teacher permission to beat Patrick. When asked to visit the classroom, she grudgingly complied. Each time, her appearance in the doorway caused an immediate change in Patrick's demeanor, which became passive and withdrawn, three fingers going quickly into his mouth and the other hand rubbing his head vigorously. No inappropriate behaviors were ever displayed when Margaret was in the classroom. On one visit, when it was planned that Margaret would observe so that Patrick would not be aware of her presence, he suddenly and without explanation began to tantrum. Margaret quickly burst into the room. Upon seeing her, Patrick immediately stopped, fear etched upon his little, fine-boned face.

The thread of insatiable hunger, the thread of fear, the thread of intimidation were becoming apparent to all of us who were involved. We made more calls to social services; again, they asked their question, "Who else will take him?" Sickness gripped the hearts of those who cared. While we could not change the bad beginning to his life, this was a social service placement--this was supposed to be a better place than that from which he came! Something was wrong. The system was not working. What could we do?

In September, when Patrick was three years old, he began his second year of preschool. His aggressive behaviors escalated. He threw toys unexpectedly. He lashed out at other students without provocation. Once, with four adults present and in his immediate vicinity, he threw a thick plastic cafeteria bowl down on the table hard enough to smash it into bits, sending pieces exploding within close proximity of other students. Occupational and physical therapists, speech-language pathologists, and volunteers, served Patrick one-on-one most of each day, yet no one was able to predict or stop his outbursts, which escalated in frequency and duration.

Now Patrick could not be placed in time out in a playpen because he could climb out. How could we contain these wild, seemingly unprovoked tantrums which threatened the other students? Should we build a time out box for a three-year-old? Should we close him in a room, alone? How should we explain his plaintive wails to the preschoolers and the other students in the school who heard their sad echoes throughout the hallways?

We asked for help. We called a behavior management specialist from a nearby university to observe and give recommendations. He praised the consistency with which we were addressing Patrick's behavioral difficulties. At this time, since Patrick could not be contained in the playpen, the assistant or the teacher was physically removing him from the class when his outbursts were dangerous to himself or other children. He was held using an approved nonharmful physical restraint technique. The person who trained Patrick's management team commented that he had never known of the necessity to use such a restraint on a preschool-age student. When Patrick stopped the physical aggression, whoever was with him rocked him or walked him, talking soothingly to him until he was calm enough to return to the classroom. These physical restraint techniques became necessary more and more often, sometimes occupying the majority of Patrick's time in school.

The morale of the classroom teacher, her assistant, and the outside specialists serving the classroom was sinking quickly. Those who worked most closely with Patrick were showing signs of stress. Sometimes the teacher's voice sounded angry when she spoke to Patrick. Articles about the effects of substance abuse *in utero* were passed amongst all of us. Yes, Patrick did exhibit most of the characteristics described in the articles; this we could confirm. But what should we do? The few suggestions offered were all strategies that we had already tried in the classroom. One-on-one instruction, consistent responses, provision of a calm and nurturant environment, insurance of success--these were all in place.

We attended professional conferences focused on behavior management of children born to substance-abusing mothers. We attended with great hopes of hearing new suggestions, only to be disappointed when no new ideas were offered. Patrick was making no educational or social progress, and surely that of his classmates was being hindered. Margaret insisted that we were too soft on him and again offered us her permission to beat him. When she came to school and publicly beat him because she was tired of the teacher's notes, social services was notified and the decision was made not to invite her back into the classroom.

We hired an assistant for Patrick so that the programs of the other students could continue with less interruption. At this point, however, the tension was apparent in the entire classroom. His classmates may have been young and developmentally delayed, but they too were aware that at any moment there could be an outburst that would set everyone on edge, if not place them in danger of physical harm. We trained the teacher's assistant to react consistently to Patrick's inappropriate behaviors--to ignore those that could be safely ignored; redirect him from frustrating activities; restrain wild, aggressive behaviors; and provide loving, calm reassurance when the tantrums subsided. Because Patrick was spending increasingly longer times out of the classroom, we supplied the assistant with puzzles and activities that were appropriate to Patrick's ability and would not cause frustration. Food was always available, as Patrick's appetite in school appeared greatly out of proportion for his size. He often ate three bowls of cereal with milk and fruit as soon as he got off of the school bus and was hungry enough to eat another substantial meal an hour later. We kept social services abreast of the problems through frequent phone calls and letters documenting our concerns.

15

In February, Patrick was moved to another preschool class in the same building. This class had older students who were bigger and more able to defend themselves. We thought that Patrick might be less likely to strike out at larger, more verbal students. We encouraged him to use his words to discuss his anger or frustrations. A short "honeymoon" period quickly gave way to the same aggression inflicted upon these students. Bigger or not, no one wanted to take on Patrick, and the second class began to suffer from the tension of never knowing when toys would be flung across the room or someone would be kicked, bitten, or pinched.

On one visit to the second classroom, I sat and worked at a pegboard with Patrick. He had chosen this activity and was happily and ably placing pegs in the holes when, without explanation and quicker than I could react, he picked the entire wooden board off of the table and flung it like a discus across the room. Pure luck would have it that no little heads were in the path of this flying object. Patrick's response to my calm statement, "This was not what we do with the pegboard," was to begin to flail wildly at me with his little fists. I was the one to take him from the room and restrain him for 25 minutes as he screamed and head-butted me. All the while, I repeated, "You're a good boy, and I'll let you go as soon as you stop hitting" in the calmest voice I could muster, my heart pounding near to breaking, my mind racing as I fought back the tears for this tiny, fragile being so full of anger and pain. When he finally stopped fighting, the little body slowly slackening, I held him and rocked him until he nestled into me like an infant. Who had ever nurtured this little boy, I wondered? Who had ever held him and let him feel the love that all humans need to feel? And, looking to the future, who would ever love him enough to make this pain go away?

That school year ended with no problems solved. There were no solutions, only increasingly serious problems. The entire elementary school in which the preschool program was housed had been negatively affected by Patrick's loud and obvious presence, and two classes of preschoolers were visibly tense and frightened by this poor little boy. No help was forthcoming from his foster mother, and social services refused to respond to our pleas for consideration of the appropriateness of his placement with Margaret. I had learned that one of Margaret's teenaged sons had been identified as emotionally disturbed and that there was documentation that he had exposed himself to other boys in the school bathroom. Questions of possible sexual abuse were constantly in my mind, but this was confidential information and I could not use it against his foster family. All summer I considered what to do for this disturbed youngster.

Patrick was placed on the caseload of a preschool teacher who was the mother of three young boys. She was experienced in preschool and emotional disturbance and, although I hesitated to break the news of her most challenging student to her, when I told her she did not wince at serving him. Because she was the third preschool teacher in that elementary school, she was completely familiar with the problems that Patrick presented. The plan that we developed was that she would work with Patrick in his home for a short period in order to minimize his jealousy of other students' relationships with the teacher and to minimize his frustrations with learning tasks. He would begin to attend school gradually, and his time would be increased as he exhibited the ability to cope with classroom requirements. The second part of the plan called for a full evaluation by a local child development clinic, which we hoped would provide suggestions for successful integration of Patrick into the preschool program.

I met with Margaret in her home to introduce this plan. What I encountered on my first visit was a hostile woman who criticized the school system for being "too soft" with Patrick. While she yelled at me, Patrick stood in the corner of the neat, clean living room sucking his three fingers and rubbing his head. When I initiated conversation with Patrick, whom I had now known for almost two years, he only looked sheepishly at Margaret. "Say something to her!" she shouted at Patrick, which he did. I could extract no spontaneous conversation from him, nor would he come near me. Likewise, he did not enter Margaret's physical space, remaining far off in the corner, three fingers in mouth, hand rubbing head. The living room contained a white sofa and two white chairs (spotless), a glass coffee table, and other tables laden with small china knick-knacks. There were no toys in sight. The only other rooms in the house, which I did not enter, were the kitchen and bedrooms. I knew from past reports that Patrick shared Margaret's bedroom; she was a single parent. There were no children's toys in the yard.

In Patrick's presence, Margaret complained loudly that she might give him up because she didn't get enough money to keep him. I silently prayed that she would do just that. This very large (fat) woman also complained that this very frail little boy--below the fifth percentile for weight for his age--was eating her out of house and home. I tried to be direct and explained that his need for food was perhaps related to his need for nurturance, as he had been abandoned by his mother. I tried to explain how disturbed we felt his behavior to be and how deeply he seemed to need security. I tried, but I, like Patrick, was intimidated by this loud, mean woman who sat yelling back at all of the points that I tried to make. Without contradicting her, I let her lecture me as to how all of Patrick's problems stemmed from his first few months with his natural mother. I didn't tell her what I believed--that she was equally, if not more responsible than his natural mother for his disturbed behavior. I left grimly satisfied that I had gotten permission to implement the plan for home-based education, hopeful that a new strategy would make a difference. Margaret had also agreed to request a full evaluation for Patrick from the local child development agency and I, naively, hoped that help would be forthcoming from these experts.

My dual plan was a dual failure. The new teacher, Caitlin, was unable to establish any rapport with Patrick in his home due to Margaret's interference. He was compliant but non-interactive, sucking those three fingers and vigorously rubbing his head almost non-stop. Even when Margaret was out of sight, his glance stayed fearfully in the direction to which she had gone. She might go out of sight, but she was always within hearing range, ready to shout at either Patrick or Caitlin.

The report written by the local child development clinic documented that Patrick vacillated between two emotional/behavioral styles, at times being shy, quiet and withdrawn and at other times exhibiting aggressive, destructive, and demanding behavior. Although they noted that this behavior is typical of a young child who has been traumatized, they did not take on the larger issue of whether the trauma was in fact on-going. Margaret and Patrick were observed in a separation-reunion procedure conducted to examine Patrick's attachment to his mother. It was noted that Margaret made no attempt to include Patrick, nor did she encourage him in any of his own play. The interactions clearly reflected Patrick's submission to his foster mother's goals as he worked hard to please her and follow her lead. Their interactions did not afford Patrick the opportunity to gain experience with moderate, reciprocal, and supervised amounts of control over his behavior. Patrick would benefit from a gradual transfer of some power from Margaret to teach him to control his own behavior according to acceptable limits. His behavior revealed a strong need for adult attention, nurturance, and physical contact. He would benefit, the report concluded, from a great deal of physical affection, emotional support, and confidence-building praise and encouragement.

We knew what Patrick needed--had known this before the report was written. What were their recommendations regarding school? That we continue with our services and our plan for reintegration into the preschool class. That was all that they wrote! As we feared, the changes we wanted lay in Margaret's hands. Family and individual therapy were also recommended. She refused. I contacted social services. This time I wrote a pleading three-page letter to the director of the child protective services division begging for reconsideration of Patrick's placement with Margaret. I asked that they exert pressure on Margaret to take part in the recommended counselling. I wrote painstakingly, attempting to emphasize the extreme seriousness and uniqueness of this situation. Six weeks after I mailed the letter, a caseworker called to ask if I wanted to lodge a complaint! I was both outraged and outspoken. She said that she would investigate and get back to me. She never has.

I called the health department to report that Patrick seemed to be losing weight. The public health nurse who had originally referred him said that he had always been a "red flag case", but that Margaret had stopped bringing him in for scheduled physicals. I wondered how that happened with a "red flag case" but was satisfied with the knowledge that the nurse guaranteed me that she would send a van out to pick him up for his physical if Margaret was uncooperative. The van was used. The sight of Patrick's bony frame brought tears to her eyes, the public health nurse soon reported. He was to be hospitalized for failure to thrive. If non-medical causes of failure to thrive could be proven, there would be grounds for social services to remove Patrick from Margaret's home. Horribly, I prayed that Patrick would be found to be malnourished!

I am not certain of what was found in the hospital, as I was curtly informed by the hospital social worker that without a release from Margaret he could tell me nothing. Margaret refused to sign a release. Patrick is still skinny, Margaret is still fat, nothing has changed.

As his third year of preschool ends, Patrick attends only three days a week for an hour and a half each day. Margaret is often not home when the car brings Patrick home from his shortened day at school. Then he must be driven back to school and the teacher must spend time on the telephone tracking Margaret down. If Patrick's demeanor has changed in any way, it has become sadder and more withdrawn. On a recent visit to the classroom, I observed Patrick unexpectedly walk over to the slide and lay his little head down and sob. Defeat marked his shaking little form. His teacher held him gently and I left, tears rolling down my own cheeks for the boy that I don't know how to help.

Questions for Reflection

What are educators' legal and ethical duties in cases like Patrick's? Given what you know about this case and Candace's frustration, what would you suggest she do next?

What aspects of this case illustrate what has been called the "new morbidity"? (Hallahan & Kauffman, Chapter 2)

To what extent might Margaret's attitudes and discipline of Patrick be explained by cultural factors? Could Margaret's approach to dealing with Patrick be justified as culturally acceptable and appropriate? (Hallahan & Kauffman, Chapter 3)

Early childhood special education is supposed to involve collaboration of families and all service agencies working with the child. Where did the problem lie in the failure of individuals and agencies to work together for Patrick's benefit? (Hallahan & Kauffman, Chapters 2 and 12)

Based on the information in this case, do you think Patrick's teachers were using appropriate behavior management procedures? Can you make any suggestions for improvement in their methods? (Hallahan & Kauffman, Chapter 6)

Do you think Patrick fit the definition of a child with a disability? If not, how would you define his problems? If so, what do you think were Patrick's most significant disabilities?

DESMOND, THE SWORD IN MY SIDE

Louise Denny

It was 8:00 P.M. on an early January evening. Between the raindrops on the windshield and the tears in my eyes, I could barely see the road. I cried all the way home from school again. The thoughts of my father would not leave my mind. He had died unexpectedly three weeks before Christmas. The holidays had been very difficult, and I had actually been looking forward to returning to school. I kept telling myself that things would get better once I was back into a routine, but I was wrong.

The elementary school where I worked was in a unique location between an affluent neighborhood and a poor area. The school enrolled students of varied ethnic origins: European, African, Hispanic, and Asian. The students' socioeconomic levels ranged from very low to very high. My self-contained class of mildly mentally retarded students reflected this diversity. I had seven boys and six girls ranging in age from 7 to 11 years of age. Some were African American. I had one boy with Down Syndrome who was the son of a United States Senator, one girl whose father was very successful in business, and three children from the near-by army base. Several of my students lived in trailer-homes or old, run-down apartments. and some of these childrens' parents were not working and were on welfare.

I was so proud of the accomplishments of my students--well, 12 of them. I felt that they were doing the best work possible and were growing academically, socially, and emotionally. We worked together nicely, and I felt so fortunate to have such a delightful class.

Yet, one of my students was extremely different from the rest. Desmond Brown was a nice looking nine-year-old African American boy, always clean and dressed in style from head to toe. Although he lived in a poor area, his mother was presently employed. Consequently, he did have a slight economic advantage over the other children in the apartment complex where he lived. Yet Desmond was a very unhappy boy who was angry at the world. His brown eyes were full of hatred, and he enjoyed glaring at the other children, at my aide, and at me. His look frightened us, and he knew it. He frequently poked, pushed, called names and made fun of innocent students for no apparent reason. He moved about restlessly in his desk while working on an assignment, sighing and mumbling under his breath. Naturally, when the other students glanced at him he would immediately yell out, "He's lookin' at me!" or "What's you lookin' at, stupid?" He refused to participate in classroom activities because, as he put it, "they're dumb." He spent much of his time at his desk isolated from the rest of us.

At the beginning of the year, Desmond was on the same behavior plan as the rest of the children. The rules, stickers, weekly behavior reports, and special treats were working for the entire class--except for Desmond. He was simply not interested in stickers that had dinosaurs on them and said, "DYNAMITE!" Nor was he impressed by the baseball cards, plastic race cars, or other little trinkets that children usually liked. I tried to find more exciting stickers and "cooler" rewards, yet nothing seemed to interest Desmond. His behavior was becoming increasingly more difficult to manage, so I had to follow through with the consequence of sending poor behavior reports home on Fridays. Yet he was not phased by these notes, nor was his mother. She simply signed the reports, and Desmond returned them on Mondays. When I asked him what his mother had said about the negative notes, Desmond simply replied, "nothin'."

As the weeks passed, I realized that Desmond's behavior was significantly interfering with his academics. Desmond had an academic advantage over the rest of the class. He was working approximately one grade level below his age peers in regular classes in both language arts and math skills, whereas my other students were at least two years below grade level in all areas. Academics were Desmond's strength, and I did not want his achievement to suffer due to his poor behavior.

I made numerous calls to Mrs. Brown and tried repeatedly to explain my concern about Desmond. Every time we spoke, Mrs. Brown assured me that she would talk to Desmond and praise him for good schoolwork and positive behavior reports, or punish him for weak schoolwork and negative behavior reports. Yet as time went by, I realized that she was not consistent and that I could not count on her to help me with this problem.

I decided that I needed more information on Desmond's family, so I called Mrs. Lee, my special education supervisor. She informed me that confidential records were kept at the area office building and that I was welcome to read Desmond's file there.

The next afternoon, I met Mrs. Lee at the Area Office. As she handed me Desmond's file, she leaned towards me and quietly said, "You may as well know that there have been rumors regarding Mrs. Brown. Evidently she has had numerous men in and out of her apartment, but nobody knows whether it's for business or pleasure. Nothing official is in the file, though." I was so surprised that I couldn't think of anything to say except, "Thank you." As I sat down and proceeded to read the family case history I became more and more upset.

The papers stated that Mrs. and Mr. Brown were divorced and that Mr. Brown was in the Army, living in another state. There were also hand-written notes from Desmond's previous teacher. She had documented some behavior problems and specific quotes from Desmond. One particular note described a morning that Desmond came into school looking tired. When his teacher asked if anything was wrong, Desmond replied, "I didn't get no sleep

21

'cuz my mama was havin' another party." The teacher reported another problem that had occurred on Fathers' Day. The class was making Fathers' Day cards, and Desmond became very defensive when a classmate said, "Why are you making a Fathers' Day card when you ain't got no father?" Desmond yelled, "I do got a father, and I'm gonna live with him and get far away from this place!"

I immediately recalled a similar statement from Desmond a few weeks ago when we were discussing our families. I distinctly remembered his saying, "My daddy is gonna come get me, and I'm gonna live with him." I did not know whether this was true or not. I was gaining a much clearer picture of Desmond's life and came to understand that Desmond was living with a mother who was more interested in men and having a good time than in Desmond and his little sister.

The first few days back after Christmas vacation were relatively quiet. All of the children were happy to return to school. Even Desmond was in pretty good spirits, and I actually thought that we might have a calm remainder of the year.

The fourth day after Christmas, everything exploded. I was in the back of the room reading a book with three children when I heard a blood-curdling scream from Bobby. I turned around to see Desmond standing over Bobby, who was sitting in his desk. Desmond had his arm up in the air and was tightly holding a sharpened pencil in his hand. He was grasping it like a weapon and was ready to swing down and stab Bobby. I screamed, "Desmond!", leaped from my chair, and ran frantically over to the boys. My scream startled Desmond. He stopped for a moment to look at me. He then raised his arm higher. I reached him just as he was about to strike Bobby. I caught the pencil, but not in a strong grip; I had only caught it with three fingers. Desmond and I struggled over the pencil, and he grabbed my free pinky finger and bent it back until I thought it would snap. I finally let go of him but was able to confiscate the pencil with my other hand. I grabbed his arm tightly and pulled him to the other side of the room. I was shaking and so upset that I could hardly speak. He was glaring at me and seemed pleased to know that he had rattled me.

I immediately began to scold Desmond. "Don't you know how badly you could have hurt Bobby?" I screamed. Before he had a chance to reply, I went on, "Your behavior is unacceptable, and I will not tolerate it anymore in my classroom!" My voice was cracking and my heart was racing.

Fortunately, the principal, Dr. O'Brian, had heard the commotion from the hallway and entered the classroom. She saw the fear and anger in my face as I escorted Desmond to her. To her "What's wrong?" my only response was, "Here, take him."

Dr. O'Brian and I had a good working relationship. I did not bother her with my discipline problems, so she knew that this must have been serious. As Dr. O'Brian firmly escorted Desmond out of the classroom, she turned to me and said, "Come down to the office as soon as possible."

22

Meanwhile, my aide, Stacie Keller, had skillfully calmed Bobby and kept the other children together and in reasonable control. Many of them were subdued purely due to shock. I praised the children for being so good during this incident and checked on Bobby, who all-in-all seemed all right. I then explained that we were going to stop our work for now and Mrs. Keller was going to read a couple of stories while I went down to the office. I winked at Stacie, and she smiled as if to say, "Everything's O.K. here; go on down to the office."

As I walked down the halls, I took deep breaths and reminded myself to stay calm. I found Desmond and Dr. O'Brian in her office. She looked relieved to see me and immediately demanded to know what had happened. Dr. O'Brian had asked Desmond numerous times, but he would not talk. So I explained the whole story to Dr. O'Brian as Desmond burned holes into my eyes with his hateful stare.

Dr. O'Brian was upset and told Desmond that his behavior was terrible. She insisted on calling Mrs. Brown to inform her of the situation. Although I appreciated her efforts, I knew the phone call would not make a difference. Still, I thanked Dr. O'Brian for her time and guided Desmond back to class.

The remainder of the day was quiet. After school I approached the counselor, Helen Tarr, and briefly explained the problem. I asked her to speak with Desmond to get a sense of his emotional state. Helen agreed to see Desmond, but she made it clear that she had a heavy case load and could not commit to more than one session now. I was relieved to know she would speak with him and was in hopes of some new, enlightening answer to this miserable situation. In addition, I decided to devise a special contract with Desmond to improve his behavior.

The next morning as soon as Desmond got off the bus, I spoke with him privately. I began by saying, "Desmond, I feel badly about what happened yesterday. I want to work with you and help you. Let's develop a special contract just between the two of us. It would be a special way of helping you behave in class and then you would receive a neat reward for your hard work. What reward would you enjoy?"

Desmond looked at me blankly.

I said, "What is something you like to do?"

"I like goin' to Chuck E. Cheese and eatin' pizza and playin' the video games there."

O.K., I thought, now we're getting somewhere.

After a little more discussion, we set up a contract and agreed that every day Desmond obeyed the class rules he would get a point. Once Desmond acquired 14 points, he would be awarded a check for 10 dollars to be used for pizza at Chuck E. Cheese. In addition, whenever I caught Desmond on task (doing his school work), I would give him a token to use on the video machines at Chuck E. Cheese. We made it official by signing our names.

I then explained that Mrs. Tarr would like to chat with him this morning and would pick him up sometime before lunch. Desmond raised an eyebrow; he knew it had to do with yesterday's outburst. Still, he said nothing and wondered back to his desk, deliberately barging into Pete as he walked by.

I did not get a chance to speak with Helen until after school. She reported that they had a pleasant conversation and that although Desmond was not overly friendly, he was polite and well-mannered. She saw no need to visit with him again.

Maybe I was over-reacting. Maybe there was nothing seriously wrong with Desmond. After all, what did I know? I was merely a first-year teacher, and all of my training was in the area of mild mental retardation. I had only studied emotional disturbance for one week in my Introduction to Exceptional Children class. Furthermore, the eligibility committee was a group of experts in the field of special education. They had placed Desmond in my room; therefore, he must be mildly retarded. But why could he do school work that was harder than my other students' work? Why did he get my jokes and the other kids didn't? Why did he understand new concepts that went right over my other kids' heads? Oh well, Helen should know best; after all, she had worked with these children for 14 years. I considered the matter closed and decided to concentrate on the new contract.

The contract was working unbelievably well. Desmond was earning points and tokens, and his mother promised to take him to Chuck E. Cheese. Within two weeks, Desmond had acquired enough points for the pizza dinner and an abundance of tokens to use on the video machines. On Friday I sent a check home with him for him and his mother to use at Chuck E. Cheese.

I arrived at school Monday morning anxious to hear all about Desmond's trip to Chuck E. Cheese. He came into the classroom pushing and shoving with an agitated look on his face.

"How was your pizza, Desmond?"

"We didn't go cuz my mama didn't have time."

My heart sank. Then my blood began to boil. I tried to reassure him that they would go this week, but Desmond didn't buy it. He threw his coat and backpack into the closet rather than hanging them on his designated hook. He stormed around the room, glaring at the other children. We tried to carry on as normally as possible, yet Desmond proceeded to grumble and tap his pencil on his desk. Finally, I took him out in the hallway and tried to calm him down.

"You can start a new contract today and get a head start on your second pizza!"

My approach didn't work; Desmond put his hands over his ears and made ridiculous noises. I decided to let it go for now as long as he would return to the classroom, sit down, and not bother the other children.

24

The winter weeks dragged on and on. The contract was no longer effective, and Desmond's behavior was deteriorating before my very eyes. He was draining every ounce of energy from me. I tried to talk to the school psychologist, but he too was overwhelmed with the number of children he was scheduled to see and test. Furthermore, Desmond had just undergone a battery of assessments last spring before he was placed in my classroom. He was the last child the psychologist had time to think about. So there it was--I was on my own. No one took Desmond's behavior seriously, which convinced me that I didn't know anything about children with disabilities. In addition, I was still depressed over my father's death. All I could do now was hope and pray we could get through the school year.

Then it happened; I experienced the worst day of my teaching career. It was a fine spring morning, and everything had been going unusually smoothly. Desmond was in the back of the room playing with Harriet, the class guinea pig. She was making little noises, and I was thrilled to see Desmond interested in her. He had never had any contact with Harriet before, and I was ecstatic to think that he was intrigued with her. Maybe he had found something to love and care for. Maybe this would help him work through his problems. Desmond was back there past the allotted time for "Harriet visits," but I let it go because he seemed so contented. About 15 minutes had passed before Sherry joined Desmond and Harriet.

Two seconds later, Sherry came running up to me, screaming, "Miss Denny, there is something wrong with Harriet!" We walked back to find Harriet lying limp and lifeless in her cage. As I stared at Harriet, sadness overcame me, and I explained that she was sick and we should not disturb her.

Fortunately, it was time for P.E., so the children lined up at the doorway. Desmond was the last one in line. As I looked his way a sick smile slowly spread across his face. He looked at me through crazed eyes and said in a low, wicked voice, "She's dead."

Chills ran up and down my spine as I turned around and lead my class to the gym.

Questions for Reflection

Some teachers prefer not to read the records of their students because they believe the information may bias them; they prefer to form their own opinions and ways of dealing with students based solely on their own interactions and observations. To what extent, if any, do you think Louise was biased by what she found in Desmond's records?

Louise was quite disappointed or "put off" by Desmond's mother's behavior. To what extent do you believe Louise's reaction was a result of her lack of understanding or attention to a cultural difference? (Hallahan & Kauffman, Chapter 3)

Louise seemed to believe that because she was teaching a class designated for students with mild mental retardation she would not have a student with emotional disturbance in her class. How do you evaluate her assumption, given what you know about (1) the relationship between mental retardation and emotional or behavioral disorders and (2) the requirements of the Individuals with Disabilities Education Act (IDEA)? (Hallahan & Kauffman, Chapters 1, 4, and 6)

Louise stated, "No one took Desmond's behavior seriously, which convinced me that I didn't know anything about children with disabilities." Do you think Louise was over-reacting to Desmond's behavior, or should his behavior have been a matter of serious concern? Why? (Hallahan & Kauffman, Chapter 6)

How do you think Louise should respond to the last incident involving Harriet?

TELL ME IT'S NOT TRUE!

Sally North

We first met, Kelly and I, at Bower Elementary, just across the street from where I taught--Cruickshank Middle School. I had a very close relationship with Martha Comino, the teacher of students with mild mental retardation at this feeder school from which most of the students in my self-contained class came. Martha and I frequently got our classes together for holiday parties, special school functions, and field trips. I had also established a peer tutoring group of four students who went over to Kirk each day for 45 minutes to tutor their former, younger classmates. Each day, they came back with stories about Kelly's inappropriate behaviors. My students assured me that I would never be able to control Kelly once she came over to my classroom, so I could hardly wait to meet this little terror!

Martha and I agreed to co-host a peer tutoring winter holiday party. I brought my students and some goodies for the event. When I walked through the classroom door, a pubescent, nine-year-old, tousle-haired female marched over to me and immediately told me where to place my goodies. In the background, Martha was saying repeatedly, "Kelly, sit down." This request fell on deaf ears. Kelly continued giving me orders and making comments. She told me where to place my coat, demanded to know my name. She commented on my hair style and shape. And she wanted to know why had I chosen to bring these goodies to her party because she did not like most of what I had brought. By this time, I was more than a bit put off by Kelly's behavior and asked her--with my sternest look--to please return to her seat as requested by her teacher. In no uncertain terms, Kelly informed me, "You can't tell me what to do! You ain't my teacher!" By this time, Martha had given her other students chores to complete so that she could come over and make sure that Kelly went to time-out in another area of the room. I was shocked. My first thought was, "I am so glad that I don't have to deal with that little pistol on a daily basis!"

Two years later, there I was, face-to-face with Kelly. She had passed to the sixth grade and was now a student in my class--she was now mine, all mine.

From all appearances, Kelly had changed. She was very well developed for an 11-year-old. Her over bite was worse, her blond hair was longer and thicker, and she was almost as tall as I. Once she opened her mouth, however, I knew that she was still the same. I now had to deal with my feelings of "I can't wait until 3:25 comes, and I can send you home."

In the sixth grade, Kelly continued exhibiting many of the passive aggressive behaviors that Martha had forewarned me about. In fact it appeared that these behaviors got worse once Kelly entered middle school. She was stubborn, tried to control children and authority figures, defaced property when she could not get her way, disrupted class discussion surreptitiously, literally dragged her feet when asked to relocate, and made annoying noises of many kinds (e.g., scratching her barrette on the table, fastening and unfastening velcro on her notebook, zipping and unzipping purses or knapsacks). While being reprimanded, Kelly simultaneously continued doing inappropriate behaviors and explained why she thought the behaviors were perfectly fine and necessary. Without asking permission, she often abruptly got out of her seat--to go sharpen her pencil, help another student, get something off my desk, or retrieve a peer's belonging off the floor. Kelly constantly made unsolicited comments whenever I was talking to another student. She interjected her opinions, turned the conversations around to be about her, or even told me what I should say in response to the student's question or problem. Meanwhile, the other student almost always got irritated and told her to shut-up and mind her own business. This typically led to a verbal or physical altercation between the two of them.

Kelly physically resembled a much older teenager than her peers in the sixth grade. Many of her behavior problems stemmed from other students' comments on her shapely appearance. At times, Kelly said the girls were talking about her, staring at her, or telling lies about her. She accused the boys of the same things, in addition to fondling her in the hallways, on the bus, or in her neighborhood. Frequently, she made these statements without any proof, and inevitably a fight occurred--one severe enough for in-school suspension (ISS).

Whenever I visited Kelly in ISS to bring her more assignments, I realized that it had ceased to be an effective punishment. The teachers gave her extra special attention because she was in special education. She did many of her assignments hastily and incorrectly or with so much assistance from the teacher supervising ISS that it was very obvious who had really done the work. Kelly was also using ISS as a social occasion. I typically found her having a grand old time chit-chatting and laughing about why she had been placed in ISS. When it was time to leave, she would actually joke about the likelihood of her being placed in ISS again and how she would be seeing the ISS teacher and other kids again soon.

I decided to start using in-class suspension (ICS) instead. This resembled ISS, except that Kelly did not leave my classroom. As in ISS, however, she didn't have any breaks (except for supervised toileting, getting a drink of water, and purchasing lunch), she ate lunch in my classroom, and she didn't attend her exploratory or physical education classes. She completed all missed assignments in ICS, and I became her only adult authority figure. I knew that she would stay on task with my supervision, but because I didn't have a full-time teacher's assistant, most of these time I felt as if I were in prison. I resented each and every time I placed Kelly in ICS. Regardless of how imprisoned I felt, I thought that maybe ICS would help calm Kelly down and give control of my classroom back to me. When she said, "I don't like being in ICS 'cause you make me do my work," I realized that maybe ICS was really working and decided to continue using it. I did so for the remainder of the school year.

I have never liked losing control of any type of job-related problem. I associated lack of control with failure. It was apparent to me that I was losing the respect of the other students when they observed my dealings with Kelly, and I was tired of my space being violated by this girl. No matter how much I tried to see her in a positive light, Kelly still represented confusion to me. I had always taken pride in my record of not using the principal or assistant principal to take care of my behavior problems. But now that my previously successful management methods were failing miserably, I was being forced to use the school's standard discipline procedures. Kelly was causing other adults to come into my room and dictate how I should run my classroom. I stopped seeing Kelly as a little girl with a problem in need of understanding and help. I felt very unprofessional because I was allowing this situation to be about *me* and *my* need for belonging and power.

Kelly came from a very dysfunctional family. The household consisted of a mother, who was always in training for a job to get off welfare, a non-working live-in boyfriend, an emotionally disturbed older brother, a very precocious older sister (also, labeled emotionally disturbed) who was constantly in trouble with the law and school officials, and a younger sister who was the biological daughter of the live-in boyfriend. Kelly's brother and older sister lived with another relative because their mother could not control them. Most of the time Kelly was left at home with her younger sister and her mother's boyfriend in a custodial role.

Kelly's mother was very demanding and bragged about how she "handled" previous teachers whenever her children were in trouble. She always talked loudly and aggressively, using profanity and looking expectantly at my face for a reaction. She constantly compared Kelly to her older brother and sister and told Kelly that her younger sister was always more obedient, sweeter, and smarter than she. The mother made a point of telling me once, "My youngest is the only child of mine in regular classes, and she gets A's and B's." Kelly immediately chimed in, "Ma, I make A's and B's, too!" only to be told, "Shut up! You're in special ed, and those grades don't count." I tried to take away the hurt look from Kelly's face by pointing out her academic strengths, but her mother would have none of that. "Kelly's getting the easy work 'cause she acts so dumb."

Kelly started her second year with me--her seventh-grade year--more physically developed than ever, still aggressive, and continuing her many other problem behaviors. But something about her demeanor was different. She started clinging to me. This puzzled me, because there was definitely no love lost between Kelly and me. But she now sought me out every chance she got. In many ways, I had become her protector. The regular education teachers who had her continued to complain about her inability to remain on task and her argumentative nature, but they also noticed a change.

By the end of September, Kelly was getting into physical and verbal altercations again. This time there was some validity to her many skirmishes. A sixth-grader and friends were spreading the rumor that Kelly was pregnant. Most of her conflicts occurred in her regular

29

education exploratory and physical education classes, at lunch, on the bus, and during hall breaks. The regular education teachers who broke up these fights began questioning whether there was any validity to the rumor. While eating lunch in the teachers' lounge, they commented on the apparent physical maturity of Kelly's body and speculated that the rumor might be true. Finally, one of these teachers approached me, wanting to know more about what she called "Kelly's situation." I did not know of any "situation" to share information about, so I declined making a statement about what I viewed as a ridiculous rumor.

Even though Kelly talked about promiscuity, she had pretty much proven--as far as I was concerned--that she was all talk and no action. I felt that the budding positive relationship that Kelly and I had would be in danger if she thought for one moment that I, too, believed the rumors. Luckily, Kelly helped me to bring up this subject in a casual conversation. During recess, she was talking about playing during the summer in a field near her house with the boy who had been tormenting her with the rumor and his brother. She made a point of talking about how no one else was around. I always talked honestly to my students about sex, so I participated without hesitation in the conversation but also took this opportunity to ask about the types of games she and her sister had played with these boys and whether they were sexual in nature. A look of disbelief came over her face. "Stop talking nasty!" she said, visibly upset. So I dropped the subject. But I decided to watch Kelly very carefully.

Unfortunately, just watching, was not enough. Kelly had gotten into a really horrible fight on the bus, and the principal deferred to my judgment about handling the punishment. I had to call Kelly's mom, Mrs. Carrington, promptly. This call was going to be another stress producer.

Even though I had stayed in contact with Mrs. Carrington through notes, I had managed not to call her so far this year. During Kelly's sixth-grade year, Mrs. Carrington had not appreciated the many calls she had received about Kelly's inappropriate behavior. She had become verbally aggressive with the principal and threatened to "whip some butts" of both the children and the adults involved in "picking on and blaming my daughter." She was also irritated because the numerous calls put her new job in jeopardy. She was trying to discontinue her association with the welfare department, and we weren't helping her any by calling about Kelly's many behavioral offenses and ISS penalties. Mrs. Carrington constantly demanded concrete proof of Kelly's involvement for each and every offense.

I had no proof of what had happened on the bus, only second-party information, but I dialed her number anyway. When I described the altercation--by reading the discipline referral in its entirety--Mrs. Carrington became livid. It seems that the boy, Lester, and his brother had been "picking on" Kelly and her younger sister, Faith, in their neighborhood, too. I brought up the fact that because Kelly had gained so much weight, Lester and others were spreading the rumor about Kelly presumably being pregnant. Mrs. Carrington commented that another woman in the community had said the same thing to her and that "I told her off, because it's a big lie. Kelly's just been eatin' like a pig. That's why she's porked up." Mrs. Carrington wanted to know immediately what she could possibly do to stop the rumor and keep the school from calling her about these fights.

I told Mrs. Carrington that I, too, was concerned about the effect of this controversy on Kelly's academic performance in the regular education classes that were shared with Lester and in my class as well. I could not discuss Kelly's academic progress without the subject of whether or not Kelly was pregnant coming up. After much discussion, Mrs. Carrington and I developed a plan of action. I would talk to the principal and the guidance counselor about transferring Lester out of Kelly's physical education and exploratory classes and getting Kelly switched to a different bus. Kelly was due for a triennial evaluation physical, so Mrs. Carrington decided to get Kelly checked by the family doctor. We figured that a doctor's report would help to dispel the rumor. School and home life would return to some semblance of calm.

After discussing the situation at length with Lester's teacher and the principal, I was able to get him transferred to other exploratory and physical education classes. There was no way to get Kelly rerouted on another bus, as no other bus route was within walking distance of Kelly's home, and Mrs. Carrington did not have the time or the additional money for gas to take Kelly to another bus stop. So, seating was rearranged and the bus driver was given explicit instructions to keep Kelly and Lester separated.

Mrs. Carrington took Kelly to the family doctor, and with the exception of being anemic and overweight Kelly received a clean bill of health. Kelly was given prescriptions for iron and diet pills, and Mrs. Carrington was told to have Kelly's anemia rechecked in approximately three months. I was sent the written report, and the principal was informed about the doctor's findings. I figured that this written report would give us an opportunity to return to some degree of normalcy in our schedules, and I could pay some attention to my other students.

How wrong could I be! Although the exploratory and physical education classes were less stressful when Lester was absent, Kelly's mornings and evenings were still chaotic because of the bus situation. She still complained of Lester looking and whispering about her on the bus. Whenever she had to change classes, Lester or one of his friends would just happen to be in the same hallway that Kelly traveled. Kelly became afraid to come or go to class, and this apprehensiveness directly affected her work and behavior in all her classes. The regular education teachers and I noticed that she started misbehaving in order to be detained at the end of classes. Lester would be in his next class by the time she was dismissed. When she arrived late to her next class, she disrupted the class by loudly announcing her arrival, missed important directions, and caused classes to come to a complete halt while they waited for her to get organized.

The exploratory and regular education teachers came to me complaining again about these distractions, so the part-time teacher's assistant or I had to escort Kelly to and from these classes. On our way there, Lester would always just happen to be in the same hallway. Inevitably, words were exchanged and energy was consumed in keeping them apart. When I complained to the principal about Lester's stalking Kelly, I was told that there was no way to stop the child from moving to his classes. By this time, the once supportive principal was

31

deferring decision making about Kelly to me. Lester's teacher would not monitor his movements as I had Kelly's. I felt I had no alternative but to continue Kelly's "escort service."

The rumor mill had started again because Kelly was still gaining weight. When I called to express a concern for this increasing weight gain, Mrs. Carrington said that she could not afford the prescribed diet pills. She had gone to the clinic to have Kelly's anemia rechecked and was told by another set of doctors that Kelly was young enough to lose the weight without any appetite suppressants.

One day in November, Kelly was changing clothes in the locker room and was playing around, as usual. When one of our two physical education teacher approached Kelly to reprimand her because she was making everyone late for class, she was overwhelmed by the sight of Kelly half dressed. While the principal and I were summoned to the locker room, Kelly was sent into the gym for exercises. The two physical education teachers concurred that no matter what the family doctor and the clinic doctors had said, they had seen Kelly half dressed and believed that Kelly was pregnant. I felt ignorant, because I had always believed in doctors' reports; however, they were adamant that we get the mother to take Kelly back to another doctor. The principal gave me the job of calling Mrs. Carrington to ask that she come in for a conference. In order to keep her calm, I was instructed to say that it was about a behavior problem. As I predicted, Mrs. Carrington was not too happy about coming in and missing a day of work, but she agreed to come in before the school day began.

I can not fully describe Mrs. Carrington's anger. When the principal said, "If you are not willing to take her back to an obstetrician, then we will be forced to call the Social Services Department," Mrs. Carrington controlled her outbursts. Mrs. Carrington and the principal arranged a visit to an obstetrician, who was asked to send a written report to the school. Reluctantly, Mrs. Carrington took Kelly to the doctor's office.

By now, the teacher-supported gossip factory had gotten information about the goings-on in principal's office. Teachers began asking, "Have you heard any more about Kelly?" every time I entered their room to check up on my other students. I would change the topic and attempt to stick to the business at hand, but to no avail. By lunch time, it seemed all of the faculty had made their way by my room. Teachers who had never taken any interest in my students or program and had never entered my room before now came to visit my classroom. I just wanted the madness to cease!

One afternoon, Mrs. Carrington came by with the doctor's diagnosis. Kelly was seven months pregnant! The principal and I sat there dumbfounded. Through tears, Mrs. Carrington kept repeating, "Two doctors told me she wasn't pregnant, and I believed them!" We tried to console her as much as possible and assured her that she had our support. When she finally left, the principal informed me that a faculty meeting would be held the next morning to alert the faculty about the situation.

I awaited the moment of this announcement with absolute dread. I knew that after the principal made this announcement to the faculty Kelly's life would be even more chaotic. My other students were already suffering from my neglect because of Kelly's problems, and I knew the worst was yet to come. I had already felt consumed by this predicament. Now decisions had to be made about how to teach, transport, and protect a twelve-year-old mother to be!

Questions for Reflection

How would you summarize the key facts of this case? What is your perception of the central issue(s) in this case?

What problems of mild mental retardation are illustrated by Kelly's behavior? (Hallahan & Kauffman, Chapter 4)

Sex and family life education are extremely emotional issues in some communities, especially when certain topics are dealt with, explicit information about conception and contraception is involved, or the students being taught have disabilities. What problems does this case illustrate and what cautions does it provide?

Given what you know about children at risk, the "new morbidity," and disability, what would you suggest as a course of action for serving Kelly and her baby? (Hallahan & Kauffman, Chapters 2 and 4)

ONE BAD APPLE

Elaine Brown[1]

After 26 years of teaching, Elaine Brown had developed a guiding philosophy which helped keep her goals as an educator in perspective. She believed that, as a teacher, she should get to know each student's distinctive blend of abilities and set her expectations accordingly. As she expressed it, "My expectations are different, not only for different students, but for every subject. If a student has trouble in math, but is extremely gifted in English and reading, I don't expect As from him in math, but he'd better give them to me in English and reading because that's his field." As she began her 27th year in the classroom, this year teaching fifth grade, she already had a working knowledge of most of her students' strengths and weaknesses because she had taught this group as fourth graders last year. She had only two new students, William and Eddie.

William had moved to Pine County from a nearby city because his mother had withdrawn him from the class for children with behavior disorders and sent him to live with his father. From the little information Elaine could gather, William's parents had divorced when he was a toddler, and his mother was employed sporadically. Often, she and her three children slept in their car or floated from one friend's home to another between jobs. When she enrolled him in Pine County Public Schools, William's mother made one thing clear: She did not want him placed in a class for children with behavior disorders.

Elaine had serious misgivings about William being so abruptly and completely mainstreamed, but she felt she had little choice but to make the best of it. So she approached the task with the same philosophy she applied to the other students-- determine what is reasonable to expect, and then uphold those expectations while always aiming higher. With William, she found that she had to set her expectations far below the average. Although he liked to read, William's reading was approximately two years below grade level. During the

[1] This case is reprinted from J. M. Kauffman, M. P. Mostert, D. G. Nuttycombe, S. C. Trent, and D. P. Hallahan, (1993). *Managing Classroom Behavior: A Reflective Case-Based Approach.* Boston: Allyn & Bacon.

first week of school, he absolutely refused to do work in mathematics. He simply would not pick up his pencil. As the first several weeks of school elapsed, it was also apparent that he was not accustomed to attending school on a regular basis. In fact, he was absent two or three days a week.

Elaine reported this attendance problem to the visiting teacher, Jerry West, who went to William's home on several occasions when William did not come to school. When Jerry had knocked on the door, no one answered, and everything seemed quiet and still. Jerry spoke with several neighbors who told him that as soon as he left, William--who had been home--opened the doors and windows and resumed watching television. These neighbors also explained that Mr. Payne, William's father, left for work at a pipe-fitting factory at 6:30 a.m. and did not return home until 7:00 p.m. Jerry then went to Mr. Payne's place of employment and spoke with him during a work break. Mr. Payne, a small man who looked to be in his fifties, explained to Jerry in a soft voice that he wanted William to go to school. He told Jerry that he awakened William each morning; but, because he left for work so early, William was able to go back to bed and skip school. "I'll lose my job if I stay home to make sure he gets on the school bus," he explained.

When he did attend school, William was dolorous and withdrawn except when someone did something he did not like, and then he became explosive. Sometimes these temper tantrums came with no detectable provocation. It was through repeated tantrums that William cultivated his teacher's apprehension and classmates' fear of him. One such incident occurred on a warm September afternoon. The class was subdued from the stuffiness of the classroom and the heaviness of the school lunch. Elaine, perspiring and weary, nevertheless carried on with her lesson on the exploration of the New World. Without warning, William rose from his desk. Wielding the large fifth grade social studies textbook far over his head, William slammed it forcefully on Chuck's desk, who sat directly behind him. Chuck reflexively jerked his hands from the surface of the desk and pulled his torso as far back as the orange plastic chair would allow before the book struck the desk with an explosive impact.

The class froze. The second hand on the plastic wall clock ticked laboriously before the spell of the moment was broken by William who, glowering at the class with malevolent intensity, shuffled to his seat and faced the front of the classroom defiantly. In those seconds which had elapsed, Elaine realized--and she knew her students also realized--that William had had no intention of altering the direction or velocity of the textbook even if Chuck had not removed his hands with such quickness. Her mind struggled against numbness in an effort to decide what to do. At four feet, eleven inches, she was not prepared for a physical encounter with William, and she was unwilling to risk further violence toward the rest of her students. Besides, she reasoned, although William had disrupted the class, he had not actually caused harm. Her instincts told her that it was best to let the moment pass, deciding that any immediate intervention on her part might send William completely out of control.

Because William was frequently absent from school, Elaine had the opportunity to discuss his behavior with her students, which she did on two occasions. During these exchanges, she acknowledged their fears and apprehensions, and as a class they agreed to treat William carefully so as to avoid provoking his anger. They would not tease him, touch his belongings, or correct him in class if he made a mistake. These were all things for which he seemed to have a very low tolerance. Elaine also asked the class to give William as much encouragement as possible by doing simple things such as nodding affirmatively after he read aloud. She had noticed that he seemed heartened by such approval, and she wanted to take advantage of this to make him feel a part of the class and feel better about himself.

Elaine took comfort in the trust she was able to achieve with this group of students. The bond she had established with them last year now stood them in good stead. This is not to say that the students became less frightened of William; they did not. What they did become, however, was much more astute in reading him and knowing when and how to hide their fear. Elaine quietly observed these developments with a mixture of pride and sorrow. However, she felt that they were all doing the best they knew how under the circumstances.

The only exception to this cooperative effort was Eddie, a small, spare boy who seemed unable to resist attracting William's attention. Elaine believed that, in his own way, Eddie was at least as troubled as William. In fact, his records showed that he had been referred repeatedly to his previous school's child study committee because of behavior problems. His parents had refused to allow a formal evaluation by which the school could establish eligibility for special education services.

Because he was small, his behavior, although erratic, was more of an annoyance than a real problem, except when it came to William. Elaine's students were growing accustomed to Eddie's unexpected bids for attention. At almost any given time or place, Eddie would poke, slap, or punch classmates much larger than himself, apparently without heed of possible consequences. Any opportunity to get out of Elaine's eyesight provided him an occasion to provoke other students. Elaine remembered the day, that, returning from lunch, she found Eddie crawling around on the floor biting his classmates on their ankles. Reprimanding him for such behavior usually brought a blank smile to his face. Although she had attempted to provide meaningful consequences for his behavior, she had yet to find either a positive consequence or a negative one that really seemed to mean anything to him.

As with William, the class demonstrated more patience with Eddie than Elaine felt she could rightfully expect from a group of fifth graders. To be sure, some students had more patience than others. On occasion, a less tolerant student would reciprocate Eddie's most recent annoyance with a sound slap or a decisive shove against the nearest wall. Because these retaliatory acts appeared neither to faze nor to hurt him, and because they rendered at least momentary results, Elaine usually ignored this vigilante form of justice.

It was when Eddie picked on William that Elaine could not ignore the repercussions. Unlike her other students, Eddie simply did not seem to understand that he should not provoke William, nor did he seem to realize that she could not guarantee his safety when he chose to incite William's ire.

That she could not ensure Eddie's safety was clearly illustrated on a crisp November day as she led her class in from their mid-morning recess period. She had established the routine of having her class line up for water before returning to the classroom. After each student had gotten a drink, he or she was to proceed to the classroom to prepare for the upcoming lesson. On this particular day, Eddie, who appeared to be bursting with energy from the preceding kickball game, left his place in line. Escaping Elaine's notice, he whizzed past William, giving him a playful push on his way to the end of the line.

Eddie's piercing scream caused Elaine's stomach to lurch and brought her rushing past the line of wide-eyed faces. There she found William on top of Eddie with his right knee planted squarely in Eddie's spine. His powerful arms were pulling Eddie's frail shoulders toward him, and his contorted features conveyed the full force of his anger and rage. Within that crystallized split-second, Elaine could almost hear Eddie's spine snap. Forcing a sense of quiet confidence, Elaine reached out, gently placed her hand on his taut shoulder, and whispered, "William." Almost instantly, William's muscles relaxed. He released Eddie's shoulders and slowly rose to his feet. His glaring eyes refused to meet Elaine's as he stated matter-of-factly, "I'm going to hurt him." Eddie rose to a sitting position and sat sobbing on the floor as the rest of the class stood in silent observation.

Turning her attention to Eddie, she asked him if he could stand. He nodded affirmatively, quickly got up, and wiped his tears on the ragged cuff of his blue flannel shirt. Watching William out of the corner of her eye, she reformed the line and directed the students to the classroom. No one spoke.

Arriving at the classroom, Elaine went to Katherine Ellis, the teacher next door, and asked her to watch the class while she made arrangements to have William taken home. She was hesitant to do this because she did not want to compound his truancy problem, but he seemed unable to compose himself. He continued to mumble threats, and his rigid bearing led Elaine to believe that he might explode again at any moment. She did not want to risk a second outburst in one day.

Upon returning to the classroom, Elaine noticed that Eddie's tears had long since dried and his memory of the incident seemed to have faded almost as quickly. She, on the other hand, would relive those moments frequently in the days to come as she grew increasingly aware of her tenuous control over the situation. She did discover, however, that she could protect Eddie from William's assaults by making sure that she was the first to intervene when Eddie misbehaved.

Although she did not believe in paddling, Elaine found that if she took Eddie out into the hall, borrowed a paddle from Katherine Ellis, and at least created the appearance that she was paddling Eddie for his misbehavior, that William would leave him alone. "It was really easy," she explained. "I would take Eddie out in the hall, take the paddle and come somewhere near him [hit him very lightly], and he would scream like someone was killing him. And William thought I was doing my duty. I'd go back in the classroom, and William would be nodding, and

37

he'd leave Eddie alone." Although she felt that this was less than an ideal solution to the problem, her main objective was to protect Eddie from actual physical harm. This tactic seemed to work better than anything else. Therefore, Elaine resigned herself to getting along the best way she could, but she yearned for the school year to end without a tragic incident.

Questions for Reflection

Review Elaine's expectations for academic and social behavior. In what way(s) do you think Elaine's academic and social expectations for her students were desirable? In what way(s), if any, do you think they were questionable or clearly inappropriate? (Hallahan & Kauffman, Chapter 6)

How would you explain the relationships among Elaine, Eddie, and William as they are described in the last paragraph of the case? Why are these people doing what they're doing?

Consider Elaine's discussion of William with her class. In what ways do you think her discussion was appropriate or inappropriate? How would you have handled the other children's comments and questions about William?

Do you believe William and Eddie had disabilities? What do you think are the advantages and disadvantages of their placement in a special class or service by a resource or consulting teacher (consider each case separately)? (Hallahan & Kauffman, Chapters 1, 5, and 6)

Suppose that you were advising Elaine on a course of action--a better way of dealing with Eddie and William. What would you suggest that she do?

WHAT YOU DON'T KNOW CAN HURT YOU!

John McCullum[2]

When John thought about his seventh period class, his breathing became shallow and a radiating knot of anxiety formed in his stomach. This class, the only one which proved to be troublesome, consisted of fifteen eighth-grade students, seven very high-achieving students and eight who performed considerably lower academically. Of these eight, five talked, laughed, and attempted to dominate the class and him throughout the period. Although John had managed to cope with these problems on a more or less passable basis, doing so had taken a great deal of energy. John had a difficult time concentrating on his lesson delivery as he was constantly distracted by the students who seemed to want to set up a situation in which either he or they won control of the class. He braced himself daily to confront this group. He thought he was familiar with the problems and potential pitfalls in this class. But John was soon to learn that it is easier to fall prey to the dangers of the unexpected and that they often hold the most dire consequences. He was to learn this lesson from a usually quiet student in this seventh period class.

One afternoon, John planned to conduct a test review in the form of a quiz-show game. On this particular day, his clinical instructor was absent and a substitute teacher was in his place. The clinical instructor seldom if ever attended class, so this day was much like any other for John. He was accustomed to having complete freedom to plan for and instruct this class as he deemed best. Because he was given this autonomy, he chose to take a different approach with the class than the clinical instructor. The clinical instructor had usually given the students individual written assignments to complete and he used very little direct instruction or group work approaches with them. John felt that it was important to use a variety of instructional techniques for these students.

After directing the students to form groups of their choice, he began the game with the

---

    [2] This case is reprinted from J. M. Kauffman, M. P. Mostert, D. G. Nuttycombe, S. C. Trent, and D. P. Hallahan, (1993). *Managing Classroom Behavior: A Reflective Case-Based Approach.* Boston: Allyn & Bacon.

expectation that although the class would be "rowdy," the game would prove to be an enjoyable and effective review technique. Very little time had elapsed before John realized that the students had selected themselves into groups along racial and academic achievement lines. Six high-achieving white students formed two groups of three each. Only one black female was high achieving. Of the low-achieving students, seven were black and one was a white male. These remaining nine students formed three groups of three each. John knew that the white students also came from upper middle-class neighborhoods whereas the other students came from relatively poor homes. Although he was aware of these factors, he was yet to appreciate the potential volatility of the situation.

When an argument erupted between one of the students from a high-achieving group (Chris), and one of the low-achieving students (Richard), he immediately rose and stepped between them. Ignoring the obscenities being exchanged, John moved quickly to separate them because they had already begun pushing and shoving one another. After separating the students, he was able to recommence the game which continued more or less successfully until the end of the class period. As the class was dismissed, however, the two students resumed their hostile exchange at the door.

Again, John moved to intervene, calling both students back to the classroom. Only Chris complied. Richard ran down the corridor and turned the corner. Because Chris did not start the argument, and because John thought that it would have been fruitless to discuss the issue with only one of the students involved, he released Chris to go home.

In the empty classroom, John reflected on the incident. Despite Richard's academic difficulties, he had not been, up to this point, a behavioral problem in class. In fact, John knew very little about him beyond the fact that he was an academically weak student and had been retained several times. Consequently, Richard was much older and larger than his classmates. John felt that he should not allow Richard's flagrant disobedience to go unaddressed. He decided to go look for Richard. Finding Richard at the bike rack just outside the building, he approached him and said that he wanted to talk. Richard responded by jumping on his bike and stating, "I don't got time for this," as he rode away. John, stinging with indignation, immediately went to the office and submitted a disciplinary referral.

Upon Richard's arrival at school the following morning, John presented him with the referral notice and walked with him to the office for a conference with the vice-principal. On the way, John explained that the referral meant an automatically assigned afternoon detention period in his classroom for refusing to stop when he called.

Less than half an hour later, John went to the office to complete some copying and noticed Richard still waiting outside the office for his conference with the vice-principal. As he went about his chore, Richard began to make comments in a somewhat staged whisper to the student next to him. These comments amounted to threats directed toward John such as, "I'm going to break his jaw." At this point, John decided to ignore the remarks.

As he was leaving, he once again encountered Richard, who had gone to the hallway water fountain. John glanced at him as he walked by, and Richard retorted sharply, "Don't be looking at me, boy." John was becoming increasingly angered by Richard's exhibition in front of another student. Although he thought it best to ignore the remarks, he wheeled around and faced Richard. Taking a deep breath to catch himself, he slowly hissed through clenched teeth, "Go in, sit down, and don't make anything worse on yourself. Just sit down and shut up and wait for Mr. Roberts to see you." After mumbling a few unintelligible remarks, Richard complied.

Although Mr. Roberts had agreed to keep Richard in the in-school suspension (ISS) rather than sending him to John's class that afternoon, Richard showed up in class. Obviously, Mr. Roberts had bungled the ISS schedule somehow, and now John had to deal with Richard in spite of the tensions created by the situation. Fortunately, Richard remained quiet and low-key throughout class.

When John reminded him of the detention that afternoon, Richard declared that he had to catch his bus or he would have no way home. Doubting that this was the case, John told Richard that he could go home so long as he made arrangements to stay the following day. He also warned him that failure to do so would result in a rereferral and possible suspension.

John's difficulty with Richard escalated the next day during the suspension period. Ironically, John had not seen Richard in class because he had been kept in ISS. He couldn't help feeling a little resentful that Mr. Roberts had failed to keep Richard the day before and then kept him when it no longer mattered. At least, he thought, they could give me a little support downstairs. How hard could it be, after all, to keep a simple ISS schedule straight?

Upon arrival for his afternoon detention, Richard announced, "The only reason I'm staying this detention is because Mr. Roberts said I had to." When John attempted to explain to him exactly why he was given detention, Richard's behavior became erratic. A sickening knot formed in John's stomach as he realized that he was losing control of the situation.

Because Richard refused to be seated, and walked around the room striking the computer, walls, desks and other objects with a yardstick, John was forced to ask students who had remained after school to complete a project to go to the library. John told him several times to be seated and tried to explain to him why he had gotten the referral. Each time, Richard retorted, "How come Chris didn't get a referral?" John attempted to explain several more times that the referral was not given for fighting, but for running away and refusing to return. Several times during John's explanations, Richard covered his ears and began singing a rap tune. With each explanation, he repeated the same refrain, "How come Chris didn't get a referral?"

Soon, Richard began performing a rap song with graphic lyrics that detailed his plan to beat-up Chris. Several times he told John that he was going downstairs to tell the vice-principal that, "You were trying to beat me up, that you were trying to hit me with the yardstick, and that you were trying to slit my throat." He called John "stupid" and "peanut-head," declared that he hated him, and asked him why he didn't go back to the university. John began to sense that the differences in race and backgrounds had something to do with the animosity he was receiving from Richard.

At intervals, Richard pulled a small bottle from his jacket pocket and drank from it. The contents looked like water, but he called it his "beer" and "wine". Two times during this period, Richard wandered outside of the classroom. John followed him, reminding him that during detention, he must stay in the room. When Richard decided to return to the classroom, he preceded John inside, pulled the door closed, and held it so that he could not get in.

Once inside the classroom, John attempted to get some work done, but Richard's singing was too loud for him to concentrate. When John delivered a stern look in his direction, Richard leaped from his chair and confronted him. "You staring at me. Don't be looking at me. Have you got a problem?" Implicit in this confrontation was a physical threat. John sensed that Richard was soliciting a fight. His pulse quickened, and much to his chagrin, John found himself sizing-up Richard's physical bearing, comparing it to his own, inch by inch, pound by pound.

At that moment, John saw a student walking down the hall. Slipping out of the room, he asked the student to get the teacher next door. The teacher, who happened to be Richard's English teacher, was quick to grasp the situation. Stepping inside the classroom, she ordered him in a stern tone of voice to sit down. Richard retaliated with several sharp remarks. It was clear that he was ready to take her on as well. Realizing this, she went downstairs to the vice-principal, who told her to release Richard from detention.

Before he released Richard, John told him that he intended to report his behavior and to rerefer him. Initially, Richard refused to leave until he had completed his detention because he thought that John would not be able to rerefer him if he stayed for the duration of the period. Finally, John told him that he could stay if he wanted, but he would still get rereferred. Richard insisted upon remaining for the entire period.

John left school that afternoon with an abysmal sense of failure. He mentally reviewed the events leading up to this afternoon like a bad song that he could not get off his mind.

Two days later, during a discussion with the English teacher and a special education teacher, he discovered that Richard had been attending classes for students with behavior disorders for the past two years. Still, Richard had not been a problem before during this class, and John blamed his own ineptness for creating the situation. If only he hadn't...

Questions for Reflection

What did John not know that hurt him most (i.e., that caused him the most difficulty with Richard and the class)? What skills required of regular education teachers was he most obviously lacking? (Hallahan & Kauffman, Chapter 1)

Supposing that John had consulted Richard's special education teacher regarding Richard's behavior and management, what information might he obtained that could have made a difference in the way he responded to Richard? (Hallahan & Kauffman, Chapters 1, 2, and 6)

When a student with a disability is included in regular classes, who should be informed that the student has a disability? When does the teacher's need to know about the disability take precedence over the student's right to privacy? (Hallahan & Kauffman, Chapters 1 and 2)

Richard might be described as "knowing how to push John's buttons." How would you describe these "buttons," and how might John have kept Richard from pushing them?

At specific points in this case, John had opportunities to talk to Richard in a more productive way. Choose one such situation and suggest exactly what John might have said and how he might have said it.

THE RELUCTANT COLLABORATOR

Louise Gateway

I stopped outside the door of Ms. Cunningham's fourth grade classroom to put my keys away and clear my head before going in. As an itinerant teacher for visually impaired children in a six county area, I visited several schools and classrooms a day and always needed a moment to make the transition from driving to teaching. When I glanced in the door, my heart sank and my blood pressure went up. Ms. Cunningham was in front of the room leading a lesson from a textbook, and every child had a book on the desk in front of him or her--except Pete. Pete, Ms. Cunningham's blind student, was sitting at his desk with no book, his elbows on the desk propping up his head with his fists pressed into his eyes. He was rocking slightly back and forth in his chair.

I took a deep breath and walked into the room. Ms. Cunningham looked up from her book with a big smile and a shrug, chirping cheerfully, "We couldn't find Pete's social studies book!" She continued on with her lesson, completely unconcerned, while I walked over to the bookcase holding all of Pete's braille books. Each print text that was transcribed for Pete took many volumes because of the bulkiness of braille, and the regional program I was associated with had supplied Ms. Cunningham's classroom with a bookcase to store Pete's books. There were probably 50 volumes representing all his texts, and each was labeled on the cover in print telling what book it was part of, which volume it was in the set, and which print pages the braille corresponded to. I looked at the print page that a student nearby had her book turned to and rummaged through the braille volumes until I found the right one. It was indeed slightly out of order in the bookcase, but it was certainly there and clearly marked. Ms. Cunningham smiled at me and shrugged again as I took it to Pete's desk and handed it to him. I whispered the page number in his ear, and he opened his book and found the place. Pete sat up straight in his chair, following the braille with his left hand while he raised his right hand to answer a question that Ms. Cunningham had just presented to the class.

I sat down in the back of the class with Pete's math notebook to inkprint the pages of homework he had done on his brailler the night before. Once I put the print translation above the braille on his papers, Ms. Cunningham could grade his notebook along with the rest of the class. Luckily, inkprinting took very little conscious attention because what I was really doing

44

was seething and going over everything that had gone on between Ms. Cunningham and me in the past months, trying to figure out what had gone wrong with Pete's inclusion in fourth grade. This "Gee, no book!" incident was only the latest in a constant line of things preventing Pete from participating completely in Ms. Cunningham's class, and I needed to sort out the situation to see whether I was giving her too little support or whether she was taking too little responsibility for Pete's education.

First I went over Pete's history in Coolidge Elementary School. He moved to town the summer before third grade, and the advance information I received from his former school indicated that he was difficult to motivate and not up to grade level in braille reading skills or math skills. He had spent first and second grade in a self-contained class for students with visual impairments, but our region had no self-contained classes, using the itinerant model for providing services to children with low incidence disabilities. I had advised Coolidge Elementary that the best place for Pete was in a semi-protected environment for reading and math with mainstreaming into third grade for science, social studies, PE, music, lunch, recess etc. Pete spent third grade based in a learning disabilities resource room where the teacher and I shared responsibility for teaching him reading and math. The rest of his day was spent with Ms. Stephen's third grade. Pete really bore little resemblance to the child described on his IEP. While he had no terrific love for homework, he worked very hard in class and quickly came to grade level in reading and math. He had no behavior problems at all and was a popular student in Ms. Stephen's class. Unlike many of the blind children I had taught, Pete had no other "issues" besides his blindness and was a very "regular guy." Although the other third graders were initially curious and hovering, they soon accepted him as one of the crowd, and Pete had a number of good buddies by the end of the year. When we wrote his IEP for fourth grade, I saw no reason to have him spend time in a resource room, and he was placed in Ms. Cunningham's fourth grade classroom full time with itinerant services from me for 2 hours a day within the class.

My time in the room was largely spent transcribing worksheets into braille and inkprinting materials so that he would have access to everything presented to the class and so that the work he did on the brailler would be ready for Ms. Cunningham to grade. I was also there for math every day because so much of that was done on the board and I functioned as a board reader for Pete during that time as well as giving him tactile explanations of geometry, graphing and other concepts that were more visual than numerical.

I had expected a very smooth fourth grade experience, based on Pete's success in third grade and the fact that he had been so easy to fit into Ms. Stephen's class. The summer before fourth grade, I taught him to touch type and use a talking word processor so that much of his work could be completed in a format that the classroom teacher could read immediately. A computer and printer were placed in Ms. Cunningham's class for Pete's use, and he set up disks as "notebooks" for each of his subjects except math, in which he worked on the brailler. Pete was also provided with a computer at home so that he could do homework and hand it in in print instead of braille that needed inkprinting. All of Pete's texts were ordered in braille and arrived before school started. I spent five full days in Ms. Cunningham's class with Pete during the first

45

week of school to trouble shoot classroom routines (How can he sign the lunch count board? Where will all his things be stored? How can he get the homework assignments off the board?) and make sure she understood his needs as a blind student. Ms. Cunningham smiled a lot, and I thought everything would be easy.

From the beginning, everything was difficult. The reading program at Coolidge Elementary was literature-based, and these books were not available in braille. I planned to braille the novels for Pete myself, but brailling a book takes about 10 minutes a page and I needed a lot of lead time to have books ready for him. I talked to Ms. Cunningham about this when we wrote Pete's IEP in the spring and she said she could let me know the first novel over the summer so I could have it brailled before school began in the fall. After that, I planned to stay a book ahead of him in my brailling. It took weeks to get Ms. Cunningham to decide on a first novel, but by the end of July I was brailling the book she chose and it was ready for Pete in September. Ms. Cunningham changed her mind at the last minute and started with a different book, not available in braille. She apologized and smiled and shrugged, but she wouldn't consider starting with the book I had brailled. She cheerfully warned me that "I don't usually plan very far in advance, and I change my plans a lot!" I started brailling the new book and managed to stay a chapter ahead of Pete for most of the book. His family read to him from a print copy in the evening when my brailling got behind, but after spending hours and hours of my summer vacation brailling so that Pete could have a book like everyone else, I was disgusted that he and I were still struggling to keep up with the class assignments in September. I was never able to get far enough ahead of the class reading to relax, and it was a constant race to see if his next book would be ready before he needed it.

Ms. Cunningham wrote the daily homework assignments on the board before class started in the morning, and the students were expected to copy them down in an assignment notebook. I was not at Coolidge Elementary first thing in the morning to copy the assignments for Pete, and maximizing his independence meant having him do as much without my help as possible. Ms. Cunningham insisted that she didn't have time in the morning to read the assignments to Pete, so I suggested that she find a student who would be willing to read the daily assignment to Pete every morning while he brailled it on an assignment card. She agreed to do that.

One of the things that was starting to bother me was that Ms. Cunningham rarely approached Pete herself but preferred to talk to me about problems and have me deal with Pete. Several times a week she would complain to me that he had done the wrong assignments or not done some assignments at all. I started to check his brailled homework card against the assignments on the blackboard and found that he had copied many things wrong or left things off the card. At first, I fussed at Pete about this, thinking he was being careless or was trying to avoid homework, his least favorite activity. After a week or two I told Ms. Cunningham that he was making a lot of errors in brailling his assignments but that he had to take responsibility for being accurate and that she needed to deal with his missing homework the same way she would with any other student's. Pete spent many recess periods making up homework. Finally, many weeks later, Ms. Cunningham mentioned that the girl she had chosen to read the assignments to Pete had emotional problems and was purposely reading things wrong or leaving things out. Ms. Cunningham had suspected this for a long time but had let me continue to fuss at Pete and had let him do the wrong homework! She felt the girl needed something special to do and only reluctantly gave the task of reading to Pete to someone more responsible. Obviously, she didn't feel that it was important for Pete to have the work done correctly (although he was still required to do make up work on his recess time), and this was a theme that continued.

Time for talking to classroom teachers is always short, so I set up a system in the beginning of the year that I had used in other classes to minimize the amount of class time taken up by my consultation with Ms. Cunningham. I needed to braille worksheets, handouts, and other short items before she used them with the class so that Pete would have his copy. I set up IN and OUT boxes on the window ledge where Ms. Cunningham could put things to be brailled and where I could leave the brailled copies for her to pick up and use. I included order forms she could attach to the print copies to let me know when she planned to use the material and any special format instructions.

Ms. Cunningham rarely left anything for me to braille. Instead, I would walk into class and Pete would be listening while everyone else followed or worked on a paper. Ms. Cunningham would look embarrassed, shrug and say, "I guess he needed a copy of this." By then it was too late to braille a copy for him. Every time this happened I explained to Ms. Cunningham how important it was for Pete to have the same materials as the rest of the class, and for a day or two she would try to have things for me to braille, but I always felt it was a token effort on her part. The situation always reverted to nothing in the box and nothing for Pete to read. At other times, even more frustrating, I would braille worksheets and Ms. Cunningham would forget that she had given them to me. Pete's braille copy would sit in the box while he sat at his desk with nothing to read. Several times I asked Ms. Cunningham to set up just five minutes a day while I was in the classroom, during which she and I could touch base so that things would run more smoothly. She consistently and sweetly refused, repeating that she just didn't plan very far in advance and everything was okay.

I suddenly realized while I was seething and inkprinting this day in February that the problem seemed to stem from the fact that everything WAS okay as far as Ms. Cunningham was concerned. While I was struggling to fit him into her class, she didn't think Pete really belonged there and was doing him a big favor by letting him "sit in." She probably thought she was being kind by agreeing to have him there. It didn't matter to her whether he did the work or learned anything because she didn't really believe that a blind person could be a part of society. I work with blind children all the time, and it had never occurred to me before that Ms. Cunningham might find Pete kind of "icky" and that was why she stayed away from him. Maybe she always managed to assign other students to explain things to Pete or trouble shoot his computer because she really didn't want to have anything to do with a blind person herself. I had dealt with hostile classroom teachers before, but it had taken me all this time to realize how hostile Ms. Cunningham was because she hid behind that sweet smile and shrug and always acted contrite. Although it was socially unacceptable for her to say directly that she didn't want Pete in her class, Ms. Cunningham never did anything to help Pete fit in, and she constantly set up roadblocks to his success. It was this indirect resistance that I was finding so hard to counter and accommodate.

I had to admit that Ms. Cunningham had not chosen to teach children with special needs as I had and that her unstated objection to having Pete in her class might stem from that. At the same time, I was furious that a child as easy to include as Pete was having a difficult time because he didn't fit Ms. Cunningham's picture of a fourth grader. I really believed that someone who called herself a teacher should be able to rise to the challenge of teaching ANY child placed in her class--especially with all the support she was getting from me--and I had seen many teachers do an excellent job of it after an initial reaction of fear and reluctance.

I had been struggling against Ms. Cunningham's silent refusal to include Pete all year, and now I wasn't sure there was anything I could do to change things. Confronting her with my new understanding of the situation seemed hopeless--changing attitudes about children with disabilities wasn't something that happened quickly--and if Pete's presence in her class and his obvious "normalcy" hadn't already won her over, then I didn't think there was much sense in a lecture from me. It was too late in the year to ask for Pete's class to be switched to another teacher, and Pete was happy with his friends. Maybe what I needed to do was lower my expectations for Pete and Ms. Cunningham for this year and hope for a more workable situation in fifth grade.

I really hated to admit that I was stuck, but it was something of a relief to understand what was going wrong. I also had a better idea of how important the individual classroom teacher was to the success of an inclusion situation. Pete's third grade teacher, Ms. Stephen s, had sailed along with him with very little help from me; Ms. Cunningham wouldn't be able to make things work no matter how many hours I spent in her classroom or how many worksheets I brailled. I only hoped that I had learned enough from my experience with Ms. Cunningham about the qualities of a good classroom teacher to help me lobby for better choices for my students in the future. I was definitely going to be suspicious for a long time of teachers who smiled a lot.

Questions for Reflection

An itinerant model, by necessity, dictates that the special education teacher will visit the student with disabilities on an infrequent basis. What problems does this pose in this case? What are the implications vis-a-vis the least restrictive environment stipulations of IDEA? (Hallahan & Kauffman, Chapters 1 & 2)

As a general educator, what are Ms. Cunningham's responsibilities for accommodating the needs of a student with disabilities? (Hallahan & Kauffman, Chapter 1)

At the end of the case, Louise is determined to be more careful in the future with regard to the placement of her students with general education teachers. What do you think of this notion of placing students with some regular class teachers, while avoiding others? Does it violate the spirit, if not the dictates, of IDEA? (Hallahan & Kauffman, Chapters 1 & 2)

Successful collaboration between special and general educators depends on many factors. What factors might have made the collaboration between Louise Gateway and Ms. Cunningham more successful? (Hallahan & Kauffman, Chapter 2)

Louise and Ms. Cunningham were using peer tutoring as part of their plan for accommodating Pete in the regular classroom. How might they have implemented the peer tutoring more successfully? (Hallahan & Kauffman, Chapters 2 & 4)

This case, of course, is presented from Louise's point of view. To what extent do you think there is any possibility that Louise is to blame for the miscommunication between her and Ms. Cunningham? What could Ms. Cunningham say in her own defense?

Would more information about Pete's visual ability be helpful in determining the level of responsibility that Ms. Cunningham should assume for his instruction? If so, what would you want to know? (Hallahan & Kauffman, Chapter 9)

There is no mention of Pete's parents in this case. How might this information be relevant to deciding what to do on his behalf? (Hallahan & Kauffman, Chapter 12)

LEAST RESTRICTIVE FOR WHOM?

Mary Scanlon

At eighteen months old, Brian was diagnosed as severely hearing impaired when his mother pursued her concerns regarding his lack of speech development. Brian was her third child, and she knew the others had made many more baby sounds by this age. Money was tight in this working class family, but the children were properly cared for and a doctor was a necessity which they did not do without. Both parents had reasonably secure but low paying jobs in a factory in a small Northeastern city.

When hearing aides were prescribed for Brian, financial help was available from a local children's clinic. The local public school paid for Brian to attend a preschool for children with hearing impairment from the time that he was two until he was five. In that setting, Brian was trained to gain optimum assistance from his hearing aide and an auditory trainer, he was provided with individual speech-language therapy for 30 minutes three times a week, and he was taught a combination of Signed English and pidgin sign. After three years of these intensive services, Brian still had no understandable words. However, emphasis was still placed on vocalizing approximations of words, and he was required to vocalize as he signed.

The IEP committee, which included representatives from the public school, the preschool for students with hearing impairment, and Brian's parents, agreed that Brian would be placed in a local elementary school and receive the majority of his instruction in a self-contained class for students with hearing impairment. The teacher of that class would serve only one other student with moderate hearing impairment, who communicated orally. This other student received all instruction, except in language arts, in the general education setting. Brian would also receive speech-language services for 30 minutes daily. Despite the significant amount of service that Brian had received between the ages of two and five, the present level of performance statement on his first public school IEP stated that he was just beginning to understand simple questions such as, "What is your name?" It was reported that he knew manual signs for about 300 words, mostly nouns.

As the special education planner, I was the member of Brian's IEP committee representing the public schools. Although I had a master's degree in special education, I had never taken a specific course in hearing impairment. I did remember learning in my "Characteristics of Persons with Disabilities" course that deafness was probably the most difficult disability with which to live because of its affect on a person's ability to communicate. The only thought that I had given to deafness before taking that course was in playing the morbid childhood game in which we tried to decide whether, given the choice, we would prefer to be deaf or blind. I always chose blind because I was sure that my memory would suffice for my view of the world, but I couldn't imagine not being able to talk. So, with only my childhood bias for blindness over deafness and a few remembered lines from an introductory college course to guide me, I agreed with the recommendations of the experts who were present at the IEP meeting regarding the best program for Brian. I was proud that I worked for a school system that allowed a student who was deaf to be educated in a mainstream setting and felt that we were adhering to the guidelines for placement in the least restrictive environment as set forth in IDEA.

At this time, I was the only special education planner for a school system with 800 special education students. The job of chairing and completing the paperwork for all of the necessary eligibility meetings kept me in the office all of the time. I knew the students only through reviewing their IEPs, chairing their initial eligibility meetings (and then their triennial reviews every three years), and trouble shooting when complaints were made. I never had time to step inside a classroom to actually observe.

However, by the time Brian reached the second grade a new director and more education planners were hired, and I was able to begin weekly classroom visits to the four schools to which I was assigned. Brian's school was amongst those four, and I became the planner in charge of the hearing impaired program. On my first visit to the elementary classroom for children with hearing impairment, I became concerned at the extremely slow progress that Brian seemed to be making. My observation of his instruction revealed that Brian was still at a readiness level in all academic areas. His speech was completely unintelligible, and his ability to sign, with his teacher as interpreter, was sufficient for only very basic communication. I became concerned.

That same year (Brian's second-grade year), we hired Andy, who was himself hearing impaired, as a teacher of students with hearing impairment for the high school. He had been educated in a mainstream setting with hearing peers until graduate school at Gallaudet University. Andy's experience at Gallaudet changed his life and his philosophy, he confided in me. Having more time to concentrate on the hearing impaired program, I asked Andy to recommend some books about the education of students with hearing impairment. The first book he loaned me was a very dry college textbook. I kept it at my bedside from September until early December without getting past chapter one. I didn't want to learn to teach students with hearing impairment myself, I just wanted to gain a broad understanding of the methods available. Shyly, I admitted to Andy the problems that I was having in getting through the textbook. Just before Christmas break, Andy loaned me *Seeing Voices* by Oliver Sacks. This book proved to be very readable and incredibly interesting to me. It gave a clear history of the various and contrasting philosophies of Americans who are deaf. A pragmatist, I quickly took the side of those advocating manual communication. I read of the frustration of students of the oral philosophy, who might spend 10 years or more in learning to speak a few meager words, while students who are deaf educated in sign language from an early age had manual vocabularies equivalent to their hearing peers. Their reading and math skills more closely mirrored those of age-equivalent hearing students, while the academic skills of these students expending all of their energy learning a few basic words were far below that of age-equivalent hearing students.

I began to discuss my concerns about Brian's lack of educational progress with Andy. After five different observations in Brian's class, Andy requested a conference with me. When he suggested that I consider placing Brian in a residential school for students who are deaf, I was shocked. Although I recognized Brian's lack of academic progress, as a special education planner responsible for implementing the IDEA guidelines, I felt certain that a residential facility serving only students with severe hearing impairments could not be the most appropriate setting for Brian. Moreover, he was only seven years old, and he had a family who loved and cared for him, I protested. The picture in my mind of this residential facility was that of an orphanage from a Dickens novel--dark and dreary, providing minimal resources and stimulation.

A week later, Andy informed me that he had visited Brian's home. He observed a supportive home environment in which Brian appeared loved and accepted but was able to communicate only his basic needs through pointing and gesturing, as no one in his family had learned any form of manual communication. Although they insisted that they could communicate with Brian, it was apparent that this communication was in no way equal to the level of communication between his parents and a sibling who was three years younger than Brian.

I read more books about hearing impairment, I observed in the classroom, and I thought endlessly about Andy's recommendation for the residential school for Brian. Educational assessment at the end of Brian's second grade year revealed that he was functioning at the first percentile in reading, math, and written language according to an individually administered achievement test. His actual classroom performance was still at a readiness level in all academic skills.

Tentatively, I set up a meeting with his parents and mentioned the idea of residential placement in order to increase Brian's ability to communicate and learn. His parents were outraged at my suggestion, insisting that he was too young and that they would never let him live away from home. I was relieved at their strong opposition, because I was still certain that we were adhering to IDEA by educating Brian in the least restrictive environment--alongside his hearing peers--and that this was the best thing for him. When I met with Andy to tell him of Brian's parents' responses and my support of their responses, I saw anger spark in his eyes. I remember only one sentence Andy spoke in our meeting: "How can you consider this the least restrictive environment for Brian when he can only communicate with one person in the whole school?"

This question ran through my head like a mantra for weeks. All of the special education jargon and terminology could not adequately answer this one real-life question. In fact, he *could* only communicate with one person in the school, and even that communication was not adequate for anything but very basic dialogue. Brian was in a school of students with whom he could not speak and to whom he was, at best, that "poor deaf kid."

His parents, his teacher of students with hearing impairment, and his speech-language pathologist all agreed that the local elementary school was the best placement for Brian. I was becoming more and more certain that I could no longer support that view. I had to convince some of this group, most importantly his parents, that Brian needed to be immersed in a community that used manual communication in order to develop an adequate communication system. How should I do this?

The residential school was a hour's ride from the city in which Brian lived. Entirely fortuitously--and fortunately--I learned that a local church had a religious elementary school in the same town as the residential school. They transported their students daily. I had the idea of contracting with the church to provide transportation for Brian as a day student in the residential school. My special education director, aware of my concerns for Brian but unsure of the appropriateness of this segregated environment, gave me permission to approach the church with my request. I spoke to the school board, and they agreed to pay a reasonable fee for the transportation. I then met with Brian's parents to offer a day program rather than a residential placement. This time, at my request, Andy joined in the meeting.

Andy told Brian's parents of the strain of attempting for years to communicate with hearing peers and the joy he had felt when he was finally able to communicate entirely through manual communication. Although he was capable of satisfactory oral communication, manual communication was more fluid, not necessitating the intense focus required to speech-read, guess what the speaker said, and then carefully prepare each word of response. At Gallaudet, he finally felt that he was part of a community instead of an outsider. Andy's heartfelt story was the turning point for Brian's family. They admitted that they were becoming less able to understand Brian's wants and that they were witnessing more frequent displays of frustration and sadness from him. They would allow him to attend a residential school as long as he could come home to his family each evening!

That year I felt that I was sending three kids back to school in the fall--my own two and Brian. I spent so much time in the coordination of transportation and plans for the new placement that I was tempted to be there to meet the bus on the first day of school. I was as anxious as if he were my own! His mother and I spoke almost daily, and we shared our concerns about his going to this strange new environment an hour away from home. That hour ride would take him to another world, we knew. How would this seven-year-old who could barely communicate his most basic needs adjust in this new world? At eleven o'clock on the first day of school, Brian's parents were in my office. My heart lurched with fear when I noticed them. Then I looked more closely, saw their smiling faces, and relaxed as they hugged me. They had driven him to school that first day, and after his first hour at school he had smilingly told them to leave. He was already a new person, they shyly revealed. They had

53

never seen him so relaxed and willing to try to communicate. In the course of his first hour he had gone from a timid, introverted youngster to a seven-year-old frolicking with his classmates, hands flying with their messages to one another.

By October, Brian was a residential student. His parents could not deny him the life for which he begged upon his return home each evening. They could not refuse their son the full life offered to him by this new school. With the help of the school social worker, they began to learn sign language so that they could communicate more effectively with Brian when he came home every other weekend. I visited the school and witnessed growth that seemed impossible after only a few months of schooling. The bleak picture in my mind was replaced with that of a beautiful campus full of smiling faces and flying fingers. My only sadness was that I could not understand the voices I could see.

Brian's latest IEP from the residential school (for fourth grade) shows him to be functioning just half a year below grade level in reading and to be on grade level in math. His mother and older sibling can now sign to him at home. And I have learned that the least restrictive environment, like so many things in life, is not always what you first think it to be.

Questions for Reflection

How should one interpret the notion of "least restrictive environment" in this case? (Hallahan & Kauffman, Chapters 2 & 8)

Mary Scanlon had learned in a "Characteristics of Persons with Disabilities" course that "deafness was probably the most difficult disability with which to live." Do you agree with this assessment? Why or why not? (Hallahan & Kauffman, Chapter 8)

At the first meeting with Brian's parents, they became angry when Mary suggested they consider placement in a residential institution. How might Mary have communicated with Brian's parents so that this meeting was more cordial and constructive? (Hallahan & Kauffman, Chapter 12)

Brian had floundered for several years in his neighborhood public school. Some, however, might consider the decision to make Brian a day student and then a residential student to have been made too hastily. What else might his teachers and parents have tried before making this placement decision?

A decision to place a student in a residential setting is never easy, and the timing can be particularly difficult. Assuming that the decision to place Brian in the institution was correct (i.e., in Brian's best interests), when do you think he should have been placed there?

FILLING MR. K's SHOES--NOT!!

Susan Washko

"What else can I try?" The words repeated themselves in my head in time to my feet hitting the sidewalk. This evening walk through my neighborhood was supposed to be a stress reliever, but today it was just extended pacing.

Following a year as a full-time student completing my master's degree, I'd taken a job on a one-year contract, filling in for a teacher on educational sabbatical. I was responsible for teaching sixth- through eighth-grade students in high-level academic language arts/reading classes. The curriculum in each grade consisted of multi-disciplinary units based on selected literature. I liked the idea of the curriculum. I knew it would be a challenge, because all three grades contained many materials I hadn't read or used. I thought I would enjoy the age level and energy of the kids, although my student teaching experience had been with high school students.

By mid-October I felt that I'd accomplished a fair amount in getting to know my students. With three preparations, I wasn't being as creative with the curriculum as I would've liked; I was often just one jump ahead of my students in reading, and scrambling for interesting activities. I provided enrichment activities when I could, and it seemed that I filled every spare waking moment with paperwork. The sixth- and seventh-graders were cooperative and worked well, and I was comfortable enough to relax and have fun with them at times. But that eighth-grade class...

The eighth-graders were a very bright, achievement-oriented group, accustomed to being assigned 25-35 pages of reading per day and, for the most part, doing it--along with vocabulary and long-range project work--as nightly homework for just this one class. Besides other classes' work, they had a variety of other interests to keep up with. Clay, easily the brightest student, already had a specialty. He devoured at least one book each week on the U.S. Civil War. He also had an interest in reading classic literature, as did Kevin, Shantelle, and Susan. Four or five of the other girls read adult-level romance novels non-stop. Bill didn't enjoy independent reading much, but he had followed a number of stocks since the sixth grade. There was a group of boys who lived for free time to spend on their personal computers and computer bulletin boards. Two other boys were gifted cartoonists and were developing portfolios of their work. Allison had read every fan magazine article ever written on Guns and Roses, I think. The other dozen's interests were far-flung. Many took instrument lessons, dance, or karate; many played sports. They had all had my predecessor for the last two years of language arts/reading classes, and many had clearly been jolted when "their" teacher announced that he was taking a sabbatical during their final middle school year.

From the first few days of the year, a number of the eighth graders had let it be known that they resented my presence. How dare I think I could lead a class in place of their beloved Mr. K? I'd been in a class with David, their teacher, in my master's program, and I readily understood their devotion. He's bright, witty, creative, a technology whiz, a writer of songs and poetry, and has the energy of any three normal people. He'd helped the enrichment program at the school evolve and had taught in this position for five years--lived in the community for many more years than that and had quite a following. I'm rather in awe of him myself.

The sixth and seventh graders had made the transition to being "my kids" pretty smoothly, I mused. They were, in the main, enjoying the class structure and curriculum. They participated enthusiastically in whole-class and small-group reading, writing, and discussion. We'd done some skits and projects, played some games, and so on. With these kids, I had few discipline problems. With all three grade levels, I'd spent time in "getting to know you" activities. Students made classroom rules in conjunction with me. I'd written students and parents letters, enclosing a syllabus and notes on my expectations.

My student teaching assignment had been with high, average, and remedial level tenth- and twelfth-grade classes in a different district, so this year was an adjustment, but I was fairly comfortable that I had made a solid beginning. I wanted to give students opportunities to direct more of their learning around the various themes, and I felt ready to do that with the eager and hard-working lower grades. With the eighth graders, I was more reluctant to take that risk, as so far they had given me little but resistance. Was it the assignments? The particular mix of students in that class? Me?

I spent a lot of time trying to understand how the eighth graders were feeling. They'd been very successful with David and had really enjoyed him. They'd established their comfort zone, had been ready to coast through this year familiar with his expectations and procedures. They felt deserted, and their first impulse, instead of trying new ways of doing things, was to complain and compare. How was I to deal with all of that? Expect tons of questions and challenges and explain patiently, I decided. Work hard to get them on my side. Be fair. And maybe hope for a little luck?

I had introduced the first unit, "Real People," and announced project options (from material left by David) including visual autobiography, audio or video recording of biographies, and research on local historical figures using courthouse and historical society documents. To Justin's sullen, "Why do we have to do this?" I'd explained the unit's place in the year-long thinking skills curriculum strand--that was clear from the curriculum guide. But the assignment and option were greeted by "WHY do we have to do this?" from a variety of questioners. I was less sure about the why of the day-to-day assignments myself--and I guess my lack of confidence showed. I found myself trying to avoid getting into confrontations over questions clearly designed to get under my skin. I became more careful about each assignment's purpose, so that I'd be able to meet students' questions. Soon, I was tying each assignment to others in the unit during my opening minute's overview of the day's activities; then I began calling on students to make those connections. That ended the questions, but new comments began: "That's stupid!" or "BOOOriiinnng!" or "Why do you have to ask us questions about what we read; why can't we just read?" In response I pulled out all of my goals for the unit and listed them. (Thank goodness for the curriculum guide!) Foot-dragging and grumbling continued. I referred to my experiences as a high school student and in student teaching to show how these skills fit into preparation for grades to come; still there was almost daily resistance to reading and writing assignments and discussions. I didn't know what to do with this question: "When are we going to do something fun?" So I counted it a draw when I at least kept back a sharp reply.

I wondered whether perhaps some of the assignments were too difficult or my expectations too high, so for a week I consciously chose easier readings and other work. That had no effect on the eighth graders' attitudes. They remained rebellious and dour.

Expectations and grades were clearly an ongoing issue--not only for these students, but for their parents as well. To allay their concerns, I'd double-checked to ensure that students knew the "look-for's" on each assignment and project. They'd done self-assessments periodically, as well. I was surprised when the first group of eighth- grade projects, whose grades were about two-thirds As, produced requests for four conferences--all of them parents inquiring about project grades in the B range. In fact, both of Bill's parents arrived at a conference to express their concern and disappointment; they said this was the first B he had ever received. That really shook me up! Were my assignments or grading really out of line? Other eighth graders' parents called to question the use of writing groups, the directions for assignments, some quiz questions. Although I was uncomfortable with what I thought was some parents' pushiness, I tried to remain calm and professional, just explaining and not getting defensive. With each call, my confidence suffered. When I was caught in an error, I apologized and made amends. The grades for the eighth-grade students were generally good, so I reasoned that the assignments must be *mostly* at an appropriate level. I'd thrown out a quiz that most of them bombed. They--and their parents--probably just needed a little more time to get used to me. And maybe there were other things I could try to help their adjustment. But what?

Thinking that my other classes frequently enjoyed working in groups, I next considered using that option more often with the eighth graders. It seemed to me that group-structured lessons and projects might provide support and reassurance. Perhaps some of the eighth graders' resistance was motivated by worries about grades? But would groups just give them support for rebelling more against my lessons? I hoped not, and after several more frustrating days decided to give groups a try for a week. The students were somewhat more receptive to working, it appeared, when they could be with their friends. But it didn't take long for self-selected groups to raise a different concern; cliques became prominent. Bill, Dee, James, and Leigh (clearly the "in" group) accomplished their work quickly and were articulate in sharing with the class. But their rudeness when other groups led discussions or made presentations included snide remarks and outright laughter. I put a stop to the audible things quickly; they resorted to eye-rolling and suppressed giggling. Meanwhile, Becky, Anne, and Shantelle presented inaudibly; Jake, Sam, Mary, and Chrissy uniformly played for laughs; Aaron, Adam and Jamie affected boredom no matter what; and Josh was always the last to find a group that would have him. Despite the challenges of the work and admonitions to stay on task until they completed the day's assignment, in any unwatched moments Allison, Stephanie, and Susan murmured about other students' clothes and hair, while Clay, Steve, and Kevin caught each other up on their latest computer exploits. The others were less predictable, but overall these groups didn't create an atmosphere I wanted to encourage, even though more work was being accomplished with less resistance. Would my choosing the groups help?

I asked a colleague who taught eighth-grade geography and who used groups about how often she assigned them versus how often she let the kids choose. Reassured by her response, that she chose the groups the majority of the time, I mapped out my choices. Before beginning to assign groups, I decided to address the class about my feeling on this issue. I explained the instructional reasons for group-structured lessons that I expected they'd enjoy. Without pointing fingers, I cited some of the undesirable results that I was seeing consistently and my battling with them about the groups they were choosing. A few of them had the grace to hang their heads, but the rest clamored their discontent.

James made a direct challenge. "Mr. K. never assigned groups!"

"There won't be any *good* groups," Zack chimed in, "if you assign them!"

Justin's "What does she do that's good?" stung, but I ignored it.

Taking a deep breath, I stuck by my decision. I allowed that perhaps our definitions of "good groups" were different, and said that since I'd already reminded them numerous times of my expectations about group work, this would be the way it'd be for a while. They left grumbling again. Now what? Even if students in the groups I assigned could work together, would they?

The tenor of the class concerned me and was wearing me down. The eighth graders had become a constant negative in my day. I was convinced that most of the assignment options for them were good ones, answering my goals and the curriculum's. Really concentrating on being familiar with the eighth-grade materials, I was somewhat neglecting the sixth and seventh graders' progress--and I resented that. I knew the eighth graders had worked on assignments this hard or harder for David. I had his handouts, folders, and notes. I'd certainly tried a number of presentation techniques and instructional strategies. Concerns about grading had been addressed. Still, every day brought continued conflict. The only way to change the eighth-grade class atmosphere was to get them allied with me about their learning. How was I to do that? What hadn't I tried? It was clearly unpopular and uncool to enjoy my class, or to do much of anything in there willingly. How could I turn that around?

Questions for Reflection

Susan seemed puzzled about the fact that she got along well with the sixth and seventh graders but had great difficulty with the eighth graders. How do you evaluate her thinking about why she is having this difficulty? What, if anything, do you think she is missing in her self-appraisal?

What particular instructional strategies do you think might have worked better with these eighth graders?

Some might suggest that Susan was trying too hard to be liked by her students and that she should have taken a more assertive and authoritarian stance with them. What might have been the advantages and disadvantages of taking such a stance with these students?

How do you think Susan measures up as a teacher of high-achieving or gifted students? That is, in what way(s) does she reflect the ideal characteristics of a teacher of gifted students, and in what way(s) does she fall short? (Hallahan & Kauffman, Chapter 11)

Given that David is still in the area, what do you think Susan might have asked of him that might have helped her deal with her eighth grade students?